St. John Chrysostom
Old Testament Homilies

St. John Chrysostom

Old Testament Homilies

Volume Two

Homilies on
Isaiah and Jeremiah

Translated with
an Introduction
by
Robert Charles Hill

HOLY CROSS ORTHODOX PRESS
Brookline, Massachusetts

© Copyright 2003 Holy Cross Orthodox Press
Published by Holy Cross Orthodox Press
50 Goddard Avenue
Brookline, Massachusetts 02445

All rights reserved. No part of this publication may be reproduced, stored in a retrieval system, or transmitted in any form or by any means—electronic, mechanical, photocopy, recording, or any other—without the prior written permission of the publisher. The only exception is brief quotations in printed reviews.

On the cover: Michelangelo Buonarroti, *The prophet Isaiah* (detail), Fresco, 1509, Cappella Sistina, VC.

LIBRARY OF CONGRESS CATALOGING–IN–PUBLICATION DATA

John Chrysostom, Saint, d. 407.
    [Homilies. English. Selections]
    St. John Chrysostom Old Testament Homilies /
translated with an introduction by Robert Charles Hill.
      p. cm.
Includes bibliographical references and indexes.
    ISBN 1-885652-65-8 (v. 1 : alk. paper) — ISBN 1-885652-66-6 (v. 2 : alk. paper) — ISBN 1-885652-67-4 (v. 3 : alk. paper)
    1. Bible. O.T. — Sermons. 2. Sermons, Greek—Translations into English. I. Hill, Robert C. (Robert Charles), 1931- . II. Title.
    BR65.C43E5 2003
    252'.014—dc22

                                            2003003988

Contents

Introduction ... 1

Homily on Jeremiah

Homily on Jeremiah 10.23 ... 3

Homilies on Isaiah

Homily on Isaiah 45.6-7 ... 20

Chrysostom's Six Homilies on Isaiah 6
Homily One ... 46
Homily Two ... 61
Homily Three ... 68
Homily Four ... 80
Homily Five ... 95
Homily Six ... 103

Select Bibliography ... 115

Notes ... 117

General Index ... 135
Index of Biblical Citations ... 138

Introduction

This is one of three volumes bringing to unfamiliar readers a score of homilies on St. John Chrysostom appearing for the first time in an English translation of their Greek original. As one volume contains homilies on Old Testament historical figures – specifically, on David and Saul, and on Hannah – here there are a number of homilies that survive from the golden-mouthed preacher of Antioch on the Old Testament authors that the Hebrew Bible knows as the Latter Prophets (as distinct from the term προφῆται the Fathers and the creeds apply to the inspired composers of the Old Testament generally). These pieces show the preacher commenting on passages from Jeremiah and Isaiah in the local form of the Septuagint version of the Hebrew text, and along with the homilies appearing in the other volumes of this series they illustrate his approach to Scripture, his hermeneutical stance and pastoral capacity for moral admonition and spiritual direction of his congregations.

Although Frances Young tells us that "the Antiochenes were fascinated by prophecy," it is only Theodoret of Cyrus from that school who has left us with complete commentary on the Bible's prophetic corpus. From Chrysostom we have little on the prophets, and are warned not to deduce from fragments in the catenae that he completed full commentaries on them; a continuous Greek work on several opening chapters of Isaiah is of disputed authenticity. Beyond dispute, however, are single homilies on passages from Jeremiah (10.23) and Isaiah (45.6-7) – probably the readings in the day's liturgy at which he preached – plus a series of (five or) six homilies on the opening verses of Isaiah 6 at the moment of the prophet's vocation. While we would like to have further pieces of commentary from him on these key Old Testament spokesmen, we can find in these homilies Chrysostom's approach to prophecy, the prime analogue of biblical inspiration; they deserve to appear now in English.

Homily on Jeremiah 10.23

This obviously familiar and much-quoted verse, which in the Antioch Bible read as follows, "Lord, people's ways are not their own, nor will human beings make progress or direct their own going," Chrysostom relishes, suggesting he had specially selected it for the occasion. And he turns it to advantage in developing his theme of the danger of misquoting Scripture to suit one's own (perhaps devious) purposes. But he soon betrays the fact that he has lately been following a sequence of readings, probably determined by the byzantine lectionary (of which we are ignorant), for the feasts of Peter and Paul and the Antiochene heroes Bishop Eustathius and martyr Romanus. It just happens that this preacher finds the set passage for the day an ideal text for lecturing on proper and improper hermeneutical procedure.

The abuse of Scripture that Chrysostom is familiar with occurs in people's citation of other passages as well, he tells us: Rom 9.16; 1 Cor 7.8-9; Pss 10.11,13; 14.1; 127.1; Hag 2.8. But it is the Jeremiah verse that is most frequently abused.

> This saying by contrast is bandied about everywhere – in households, in market places, in town, in cities, on land and sea and islands. Wherever you go, you will hear many quoting this: Scripture says, "Peoples' ways are not their own."

What is particularly faulty in this frequent citation, Chrysostom says, is the failure to respect the context in which the words occur (a failure, incidentally, of which he can be guilty himself). More than once he lectures his listeners on how sound exegesis should occur.

> Let us examine not only this part, 'Peoples' ways are not their own,' but as well the whole context, to whom it refers, by whom, in connection with whom, for what reason, when and how.
>
> It is therefore not sufficient to say that it is written in Scripture: there is need to read as well the whole context. If we were prepared to sunder the connection and relationship of one part with another, many depraved doctrines would thus arise.

Chysostom instances Paul's advice to "the unmarried and the widows" in 1 Cor 7.8-9 as another case in point, showing the havoc that would be created if the words were taken to apply to unmarried women in general when in fact they are inapplicable to those who have vowed virginity or widowhood.

The other major popular abuse of Scripture that Chrysostom sees this verse exemplifying is incomplete citation of a text, which he sees as tantamount to "mangling the limbs of Scripture." In this practice there is a failure to respect the prophet's thought by citing only the opening clause, "People's ways are not their own," which encourages moral irresponsibility. It happens also, he says, in respect of Rom 9.16 and Ps 127.1:

> Their interest is not in this saying alone: they also relate it to others of this kind, "It is not the result of willing or acting," and then after that, "Unless the Lord built a house, those building it labored in vain." Now, they do this to make the divine Scriptures serve as a cover for their own indifference (ῥᾳθυμία), and in an endeavor to impair our salvation and hope by means of these words.

The remedy is to cite the whole verse or even the whole context.

A correlative abuse of Scripture that Chrysostom inveighs against is the introduction of elements from another source, as happens with the prophet Haggai 2.8. To the words, "The silver is mine and the gold is mine," people were in the habit of adding a further clause, "And I shall give it to whomever I wish," thus again arriving at a licence for irresponsible behavior at variance with the prophetic text. It is sheer perversity, he says: "Such is the devil's malice, to introduce harmful doctrines by addition or subtraction or distortion or alteration of the contents," when Scripture pure and unalloyed offers "norms, definitions and unalterable doctrines" for our guidance. Just go back to the context, he says, and you will find that instead of that intrusive clause, the prophet proceeds to say (of the rebuilding of the Temple), "And the final glory of this house will exceed the former."

The offence committed by such perverse abuse of Scripture in Chrysostom's view is twofold. Firstly, violence is done to the Word of God incarnate in the sacred text, a fundamental tenet of this Antiochene commentator's approach to the Bible. Every detail of the text is sacred, and requires precision, ἀκρίβεια, of the reader and the commentator.

> Hence the need to give precise attention (ἀκρίβεια) to the text. From two points of view it is a hazard and a pitfall, unless we read the verse soberly. What, in fact, are we to say – that the prophet lied? But that is perilous; a prophet does not lie: they are God's words he utters.

Secondly, the habit is simply a ruse to avoid accountability for one's actions, misquoting Scripture to abdicate responsibility and transfer it to God. Such an attitude is directly opposed to Antiochene morality, where human effort is seen to be on a par with, or even prior to, divine involvement, and therefore indifference (ῥᾳθυμία) is the capital sin. Jeremiah did not mean to give people licence to act irresponsibly. "What he means is something like this: not everything is up to us, some things depending on us, some on God … Through willing and acting we win God over to assist us." The uneasy balance in Antiochene morality between divine grace and human effort may tilt in favor of the latter; misquotation of Jer 10.23 cannot be allowed to tilt it in the other direction. That was the message the preacher wanted his congregation to grasp that day in Antioch when the liturgy offered him the text for comment.

Homily on the Verse
of the Prophet Jeremiah

*"Lord, people's ways are not their own,
nor will human beings progress
or direct their own going" (Jer 10.23).*

While some parts of this material highway are smooth and level, others are steep and quite rough. Likewise some parts of the divine Scriptures, too, are inherently obvious to everyone, whereas others require greater work and effort. When we travel an even and level way, however, there is no need of great precision; but when it is steep and narrow and leads to the very summit, with precipices bordering it on all sides, we need an alert and attentive spirit, the difficulty of the terrain leaving no room for carelessness. In fact, should one look away even for a moment, a mere stumble and the whole body goes crashing down, a mere glance into the void and one gets dizzy and falls.

Similarly in the case of the divine Scriptures, too, some of the ideas are simple and easy, and it is possible for a thoughtless person to make some headway, whereas others are quite rough and steep, and it is not so easy to find one's way through them. Hence the need to be alert and attentive when we come across such places if we are not to put at risk matters of real importance. This is in fact the reason that we sometimes gave you practice in the easier parts and sometimes led you on to the more difficult parts, both to lighten the labor for you and to dispel your laziness.[1] You see, just as people who always experience easy times become more remiss, so those constantly confronted with greater challenges give up in the face of hardship. (154) Consequently, we should vary the kind of teaching, imparting now this kind, now that, lest our mind be unduly relaxed, on the one hand, and on the other in case it should be excessively stretched and eventually snap when despairing in the face of hardship.

This is the reason why the other day, when speaking to you of Paul and Peter and the dispute that developed in Antioch between them,[2] we demonstrated to you that their apparent conflict was more useful than complete harmony. We led you along that level and rough way, but when we saw that you had grown weary, we guided you on the day after that to a different and simpler topic, singing the praises of blessed Eustathius, and after him we celebrated the memory of the noble martyr Romanus, at which the assembly actually became more joyous, the applause greater and the cheers more deafening.[3] You see, just as when someone is off-color and goes out into the fresh air, their spirits improve and they become more relaxed by experiencing nothing hard or burdensome but only rest, enjoyment and much solace, this too was your condition at that time: after the labors and hardship of paying attention like that, you went into the fresh air, as it were, of the martyrs' celebrations and had your fill of that pleasant experience in complete tranquillity. At that time, you see, there was no striking and feinting, no ducking and weaving: the sermon had the floor to itself, no opposition, unfettered, (155) free and unshackled.[4] Hence, it was more joyous and festive, and met with greater plaudits: the listeners' minds, following the words with ease and appreciating greater relaxation, were stirred more enthusiastically to applaud the speaker.

Since, therefore, we gave you sufficient relief on those days, proposing nothing difficult or demanding to your good selves – come now, let us bring you in turn to the former exercise, guiding you to the more difficult parts of the Scriptures that require deeper understanding, not for us to be crushed by weariness but to be practised in being competent to find our way safely even through these places. Accordingly, just as initially there seemed to be a kind of conflict and rivalry between the apostles, but on climbing to the lookout we then saw from there the fruit of the Spirit – love, joy, peace[5] – and the effort was not idle or in vain but productive of happiness, so too today I count on your prayers in the hope of finding everything there smooth and level and easy provided we traverse with patience and much endurance the way lying before us and are able to climb to the very top.

What, then, is the subject proposed to us this time? The verse read out from the prophet, "Lord, people's ways are not their own, nor will human beings make progress and direct their own going." Such is the problem; you for your part must now concentrate, just as you brought your interest to bear on that occasion, since far from being any less important than that one, this problem requires even greater study. Why on earth? Because while the apparent disagreement between Paul and Peter, which was not real, was not known to many, and so as a result of the ignorance the likelihood of great harm occurring was not great, this saying by contrast is bandied about everywhere – in households, in market places, in towns, in cities, on land and sea and islands. Wherever you go, you will hear many quoting this: Scripture says, "People's ways are not their own." Their interest is not in this saying alone: they also relate it to others of the kind, "It is not the result of willing or acting," and then after that "Unless the Lord built a house, those building it labored in vain." Now, they do this to make the divine Scriptures serve as a cover for their own indifference,[6] and in an endeavor to impair our salvation and hope by means of these words.

Their aim in these efforts is to establish nothing other than this, that we are not responsible for anything; all effort of ours is to no avail; futile the promise of kingdom, futile the threat of hell, futile laws, retribution, punishment and counsels. What is the point (they say) of anyone giving advice to the one responsible for nothing? what is the point of anyone making a promise to the one bereft of all competence? The person who practises virtue deserves no commendation, nor is the one who sins liable to punishment and retribution if the obligation to act does not fall on us. If people accepted this, no one would any longer embrace virtue, no one shun vice: even if here-below we were daily to sound off about hell, preach about the kingdom, (156) call to mind the unspeakable punishments and the rewards surpassing human understanding, advising, urging, piling words upon words, scarcely anyone would undertake the effort of virtue, scarcely anyone would desist from the pleasure of sinning. If you were to cut away the sacred anchor, would not the whole vessel go under, all hands eventually drowning and being lost, and many shipwrecks occurring every day? Nothing, in fact, nothing is so much the devil's object as to convince the human spirit of this, that in sinning no one is liable to punishment and in virtue no one is deserving of commendation and crown, his purpose being to slacken the hands of the zealous, extinguish enthusiasm, deepen the apathy of the faint-hearted and augment their indifference.

Hence the need to give precise attention to the text.[7] From two points of view it is a hazard and a pitfall, unless we read the verse soberly. What, in fact, are we to say – that the prophet lied? But that is risky; a prophet does not lie: they are God's words he utters.[8] Or did the prophet not lie – and so the obligation to act does not fall on us? The obligation to act does fall on us, however, and the prophet did not lie: we shall stand by both these truths, if you pay attention. Hence my showing it to be a hazard from two points of view, you see, so that by being on the alert we might finish the course ahead of us. I mean, let us examine not only this part, "People's ways are not their own," but as well the whole context, to whom it refers, by whom, in connection with whom, for what reason, when and how.[9] It is not sufficient to say, after all, that it is written in the Scriptures, nor by lifting the words out of context mangle the limbs of the body of the divinely-inspired Scriptures, and by leaving them naked and bereft of their inter-connection arrogantly abuse them. This is the way, in fact, that many corrupt doctrines are introduced into our life, under pressure from the devil for more negligent readers to give a distorted account of the contents of the Scriptures, or by adding or subtracting to cloud the truth.

It is therefore not sufficient to say that it is written in Scripture: there is need to read as well the whole context; if we were prepared to sunder the connection and relationship of one part with another, many depraved doctrines would thus arise. It is written in Scripture, remember, "There is no God,"[10] "He turned away his face lest he see in the end," and "God will not require an account."[11] So, tell me, what does it mean – there is no God? he has no interest in happenings on earth? Who could bring themselves to say or listen to this? Admittedly, it is written in Scripture; but learn how it is written. "A fool said in his heart," the text reads, "There is no God." The sentiment and the conclusion are not from Scripture but from the fool's mind; Scripture was not voicing its own sentiment, but reporting somebody else's. And again, "To what point did the impious provoke God? He said in his heart, note, He will not require an account. He turned away his face lest he see in the end." (157) Here too he is citing an impious and corrupt person's judgement and conclusion. It is likewise the practice of physicians as well, when talking with healthy people, to mention the faults of the insane and demented so as to make them more cautious. Since, then, on the one hand godliness is health of soul, and on the other hand not to know God is chronic illness and infirmity, he quotes the words of the ungodly, not for us to receive them uncritically, but for us to be on our guard. He quotes what the fool said so that you may come to your senses and not give credit to the view; he quotes what the ungodly said so that you may shun ungodliness.

Not only should a text not be taken out of context: it should actually be proposed in its entirety, with nothing added.

Many people, at any rate, bandy about some other passages from the Scriptures as well, drawing out distorted interpretations. They say, for example, It is written, If you are aflame with passion, marry. Nowhere, however, is this written that way; as to how it is written, give heed. "Now, to the unmarried and to the widows I say it is good for them to remain as I am; but if they lack self-control, let them marry: it is better to marry than to be aflame with passion." [12] Is not the saying, If you are aflame with passion, marry (you ask), not the same as that? Even if the saying, If you are aflame with passion, marry, were the same, they should not pass over a sound report of Scripture so as to distort it and replace the ideas of Scripture with their own words. But as it is, we shall find the difference to be considerable: if you were simply to say, If you are aflame, marry, you would give all who had chosen to live a life of virginity the right to dissolve their covenant with God whenever they felt the pressure of desire, to abandon that state for marriage and to forget about their former commitment.

If, however, you were to find out to whom Paul is speaking, that it was not to all and sundry but to those not yet under vow, you would be in a position to withhold that harmful and ruinous permission. "To the unmarried and to widows I say," he says, note, not to those vowed to widowhood, but to those who had not yet made up their minds one way or the other, being midway between the two positions. He is saying: Take the example of someone who lost a husband, and had not yet decided with herself or determined whether she should choose widowhood or take a second husband; my advice to her, he is saying, is that it is good to be that way, but if she cannot accept the burden, let her marry. Those who have already made a commitment, on the other hand, and have signed up for the endurance of widowhood and made their vows to God I am saying are no longer in a position to enter into a second marriage. Hence in writing to Timothy about them he says something similar: "But decline to accept younger widows: when they behave wantonly against Christ, they want to marry, incurring condemnation for violating their former commitment." [13] Do you see how he imposes punishment and retribution on them in this case, and says they are deserving of judgement and condemnation for breaking their vows to God and going back on their promise? So it is clear from this that that other saying was not directed at those under vow. Hence, instead of quoting the Scriptures without qualification, there is need to know also the persons to whom they are addressed. [14] (158)

Again, they bandy about a saying, not distorting its context, but adding something which is not in the text – such is the devil's malice, to introduce harmful doctrines by addition or subtraction or distortion or alteration of the contents. What is a verse of this kind? The silver is mine, and the gold is mine, and I shall give it to whomever I wish. While part of this is in the text, part of it is not in the text, being introduced from somewhere else: "The silver is mine, and the gold is mine" was said by the inspired author, [15] whereas the part, I shall give it to whomever I wish, is not the following clause, but is bandied about as a result of the ignorance of the general run of people. Now, what harm ensues from this case as well? There are many disgusting and intemperate rogues, unworthy of seeing the light of day, of living or drawing breath, who enjoy great affluence by causing total upheaval, seizing widows' houses, maltreating orphans, lording it over the needy. The devil, therefore, in his wish to convince people that all wealth is from on high and by way of God's gift, with the intention of inflicting great blasphemy on the Lord from this idea, took this statement made in Scripture, "The silver is mine, and the gold is mine," and added another one not found in Scripture, And I shall give it to whomever I wish. Now, the prophet Haggai did not say that: when the Jews returned from the foreign land, and were bent on rebuilding the Temple and restoring it to its former magnificence, they lacked resources, with enemies surrounding them, a great need felt, no supplies evident anywhere; so with the aim of bringing them to firm hope and of persuading them to be confident of the outcome, he said on God's part, "The silver is mine, and the gold is mine, and the final glory of this house will exceed the former."

What is the implication of this for the subject in hand? That one should not carelessly cite the verses of Scripture, removing them from their context, separating them from related material, isolating the words from the assistance given by what follows and what precedes so as to indulge rashly in slander and abuse. I mean, how is it not absurd for us, when involved in litigation in court about secular matters we adduce all the judgements and cite places, times, causes, persons and countless other details, but when the contest affecting us is to do with eternal life we cite the Scriptures carelessly and in an offhand manner? No one, after all, would read out a royal law carelessly and in an offhand manner: unless they were to detail the time, mention the lawgiver and provide the text in its entirety, they would be punished and pay the ultimate penalty. In our case, on the contrary, in reading out not a human law but the one brought down from heaven, are we to treat it with such indifference as to tear it limb from limb? How could this merit excuse or pardon?

Perhaps I have labored this point excessively; it was not without purpose, however, but to draw you away from a bad habit. So let us not grow tired until we reach the end; this, after all, (159) was why we were made, not to eat and drink and wear clothes, but to avoid evil and choose virtue by adopting the divine value system. For proof, in fact, that we were not made for eating and drinking but for other far greater and better things, listen to God himself explaining the reason why he made the human being: at the time of its creation he spoke this way, "Let us make the human being in our image and likeness." [16] Now, we become like God not by eating and drinking and wearing clothes – God does not eat or drink or wear clothes – but by practising righteousness, giving evidence of lovingkindness, being good and kind, showing mercy to the neighbor, pursuing every virtue; eating and drinking we have in common with the nature of brute beasts, and in that regard we are no better than they. But what is the basis of our superiority? Being made in God's image and likeness. So let us not grow tired of discussing virtue; instead, let us bring this inspired saying into focus, examine it precisely and learn who is the speaker, on what subject, on what occasion, to whom and in what situation, investigating everything without exception that contributes to the study.

The speaker, then, is the prophet Jeremiah, who is making supplication not for himself but for others, for Jews, who are ungrateful, unappreciative, incorrigible, due to be punished and to endure the ultimate penalty, people of whom God said to him, "Do not pray to me for this people, because I shall not pay heed to you." [17] Some say it refers to Nebuchadnezzar: since the savage intended to make war on them, destroy the city and take them off into captivity, he wanted to convince everybody that he would prevail over the city on the basis not of his might and main but of their sins, God commanding the army and leading it against his own city; so he says, "I know, Lord, that people's ways are not their own, nor will human beings make progress or direct their own going." Now, what he means is something like this: this way which the savage is treading in waging war against us is not of his own doing, nor was he responsible for this war and victory; rather, had you not given us into his hands, he would not have prevailed or succeeded. Hence, he says, I beg and implore, since you have decided this, that the punishment be inflicted moderately. "Correct us, but deliberately and not in anger."[18]

Since, however, some take a contrary view to this, and claim that it does not refer to the savage but to ordinary human nature, it is necessary to take issue with them as well. What, then, can be said in response to them? That he was praying for sinful human beings, for whom he had often been forbidden to pray. Hence he causes the city to lament first: since he had constantly said, Do not pray for them, he introduces it first in its need of lovingkindness so as to draw from it some occasion and appealing pretext to win God over to it and direct attention to it, saying, "Woe is me under your onslaught, your blow is grievous." (160) Then it says in turn, "Truly this is an affliction, my tent is destroyed, my coverings torn, my children and my sheep have left me, and are no more. The shepherds acted stupidly and did not seek out the Lord. There comes the sound of a rumor and a mighty earthquake from the north to reduce the cities of Judah to destruction and a sparrows' nest."[19] Then, after it had dramatised its own situation, he says, "Lord, people's ways are not their own." So what does that mean? because he was in mourning (someone may suggest), he introduced a pernicious doctrine into the world, eliminating our independence and saying that no obligation to act falls on us? Not at all: though in mourning, he still confirms it, saying, "People's ways are not their own," but not stopping at that, adding instead, "Nor will human beings make progress or direct their own going."

Now, what he means is something like this: not everything is up to us, some things depending on us, and some on God. That is to say, choosing the best, being willing, showing zeal and enduring every hardship come from our intention, whereas bringing them to a conclusion, not allowing them to go wrong, and reaching the very goal of virtuous actions belongs to grace from on high. God, you see, imparted virtue to us, neither leaving everything up to us in case we be carried away in our folly, nor taking everything to himself in case we slide into indifference; instead, he leaves some slight part to our effort, and conducts the major part himself.[20] For proof, in fact, that if everything were up to us, it would puff many people up and bring them crashing down, let us listen to the pharisee,[21] what he said, what heights of arrogance he reached, how he boasted, how his head was bigger than the whole world. Hence instead of making everything depend on us, he left something to us so as to find a convincing pretext for crowning us rightfully. He also indicated as much in that parable in which he says that at the eleventh hour he found people and sent them into the vineyard to work.[22] But what work could they do at the eleventh hour? Nonetheless, even the short space of time was sufficient for God to give them the full reward.

For you to grasp that the prophet really means this and is not removing independence from us, but in this case is enunciating sound values about the outcome of events, listen to the sequel: after saying, "People's ways are not their own," he immediately adds, "Correct us, Lord, but deliberately and not in anger." You see, if nothing at all were left up to us, it would have been pointless for him to say, "Correct us, but deliberately." After all, what could be more unjust than punishing those who have no say in what has to be done, and for people to suffer retribution whose way and life are not subject to their own independence? And so when he is seen to be beseeching God for the punishment of them not to be too severe, he is bringing out nothing other than that they deserve to be punished and suffer retribution; it means nothing other than that he imparts free will.[23] You see, if they had no (161) say in what had to be done, there would have been need to ask, not for them to suffer a milder punishment, but for them not to be punished at all – or, rather, there would have been no need to ask: God does not need someone to beseech him not to punish the innocent. Why mention God, when not even a person with sense would do so? So when the prophet is seen to be making an appeal on behalf of Jews, obviously he is appealing for sinners; and sin comes on to the scene at the time when we, who have a say in not transgressing the law, transgress it.

And so it is clear to us from all sources that our virtuous actions are both up to us and up to God. Such is the meaning also of the saying, "It is not the result of willing or acting, but of God's having mercy." You ask, Why do I act? why do I will if it is not all up to me? In order that through willing and acting you may win God's grace and favor so that he may cooperate with you, extend his hand and lead you to a successful outcome; if you withdraw this and stop acting and willing, God will not extend his hand, either, and instead he too will withdraw. How does this emerge? Listen to what he says to Jerusalem: "How often did I want to gather together your children together, but you did not want it. Lo, your house is left desolate." [24] Do you see how, since they did not want it, God also withdrew? Hence the need for us both to will and to act, so that we may also win God over.

This, then, is what the prophet also is saying, that good action rests not with us but with God's assistance, whereas choice rests with us and with our free will. If, then (someone may say), performing or not performing good actions rests with God's assistance, it would be fair for me to incur no responsibility; after all, when I do all I can, I wish, I choose, and I involve myself in the affair, but the one who determines the outcome does not cooperate or extend a hand, I am free of all blame. This is not the case, however, this is not the case: it is impossible that, despite our wishing and choosing and intending, God would leave us in the lurch. After all, if he urges those unwilling and advises them to will and intend, much less would he leave in the lurch those who have made a choice. "Consider ancient generations," Scripture says, remember, "and see: who hoped in the Lord and was confounded? or who remained faithful to his commandments and was ignored by him?"[25] And again Paul says, "Hope does not disappoint,"[26] hope in God: it is impossible for anyone hoping in the Lord with their whole mind and contributing all they have to fall short of their goal. And again, "God is faithful, and he will not allow you to be tempted beyond (162) your capability; instead, along with the temptation he will produce the way out so that you may be able to endure."[27] Hence some wise man gave this advice, "Child, if you come forward to serve the Lord, prepare your soul for temptation. Set your heart right, persevere, and do not be anxious in a time of introduction. Cling to him, and do not stray."[28] And another saying recommends, "The one who endures to the end will be saved."[29]

Now, all these are norms, definitions and unalterable doctrines; it is necessary to have fixed in our soul the fact that it is impossible for anyone displaying zeal, being mindful of their own salvation and giving evidence of every effort on their part to be ever abandoned by God. Do you not hear what he says to Peter? "Simon, Simon, how many times has Satan demanded to sift you like grain, and I prayed for you that your faith might not fail."[30] In other words, when he sees the burden exceeding our capacity, he extends his hand and lightens the trial, whereas when he sees us betraying our own salvation by our indifference and pusillanimity and not wanting to be saved, he lets us go and leaves us in the lurch. He does not compel or oblige, you see, and what he did in his teaching happens in this case as well: just as he did not force or compel those who went off instead of being willing to listen,[31] whereas for those who paid him heed he resolved problems and explained riddles, so too in these matters he does not force or compel the unfeeling and unwilling, and instead he wins over with great enthusiasm those who have opted for him. Hence Peter's saying, "I realise in truth that anyone in any race who fears God and does what is right is acceptable to him."[32] The Old Testament author offers the same advice in saying, "If you are willing and hearken to me, you will eat the good things of the earth; but if you are unwilling and do not hearken to me, a sword will consume you."[33]

Aware of this, therefore, and of the fact that willing and acting are up to us, and through willing and acting we win God over to assist us, and in winning him over we shall reach the goal of our endeavors,[34] let us exert ourselves, dearly beloved, and give evidence of complete zeal in the saving of our soul so that by taking trouble for a short time here-below we may enjoy the everlasting and immortal age of undying good things. May it be the good fortune of us all to attain this, thanks to the lovingkindness of our Lord Jesus Christ, to whom with the Father and the Holy Spirit be the glory, now and forever, for ages of ages. Amen.

Homily on Isaiah 45.6-7

Preachers do not generally choose the more obscure passages of Sacred Scripture for commentary from the pulpit, even if the congregation can be complimented for showing sufficient motivation to resist a counter-attraction like the races to attend a liturgical celebration. It was Lenten practice that obliged Chrysostom for one to take on the task of commenting on the text of Genesis in church, as we see in his complete series of homilies on that book and in the partial treatment in the Homilies on the Statues; but at least that text is narrative and generally less challenging than the prophetic oracles that compose the works of the Latter Prophets. By contrast, the Psalms, which have a level of difficulty somewhere between those two genres, he chose to comment on in the more scholastic environment of a διδασκαλεῖον (if we can concede that his fifty-eight commentaries on the Psalter were actually delivered to an audience, as the evidence seems on the whole to suggest). But the liturgy can at times leave the preacher no choice, as we saw in the case of the homily on Jer 10.23; and Chrysostom's commentary on Isaiah 45.6-7, which in his text reads, "I the Lord God brought light and darkness into being, making peace and creating evils," bears all the marks of an unavoidable imposition on a preacher who finds its use of paradox disarming, and who fittingly expresses some remorse for having mocked "the scholars" so often on other occasions.

And not simply a preacher: in this case it now seems clear that Chrysostom is speaking as bishop in Constantinople, giving his homily on this text during a eucharistic liturgy in the wake of an earlier speaker (as was the custom for a bishop), the day's readings comprising also the Gospel pericope of the woman with a flow of blood (Matt 9.20-22), Paul's catalogue of hardships from 2 Cor 6 or 11, and possibly Ps 137 as a responsorial psalm. Our imperfect knowledge of Byzantine lectionaries does not allow us to pinpoint the occasion more precisely. Editor Montfaucon, relying solely on a single Munich ms to which his English predecessor Savile had access,[1] which makes no local reference, had dismissed the suggestion of Tillemont that Constantinople and not Antioch was the place of delivery; and the homily's place in PG 56 tucked in beside a similar piece on Jeremiah 10.23 that is indisputably Antiochene tended to confirm the impression – an impression now conclusively dissipated. Other mss of the homily have become available with a fuller title not only mentioning Chrysostom's role as second speaker but also referring to the church as that of Sancta Eirene, close to Sancta Sophia. It follows that the homily belongs to Chrysostom's period of ministry as bishop in Constantinople beginning with his consecration in February 398.

The earlier speaker at the day's liturgy had spoken to one of the texts, possibly the opening verses of the psalm, which served as a responsorium or ὑπακοή, as Chrysostom notes at the beginning.[2] The bishop then girds himself for the task of "spreading the customary banquet" and "offering the bowl with great liberality" after an opening taste of "the honey of instruction" from his fellow. At once, however, he finds reason to skirt treatment of a text that is by any standard paradoxical and that, by its associating the divinity with the creation of evil, is repulsive for an eastern believer. So he accepts the invitation of his own comparison of banquets and brimming bowls to launch straight into a defense of the goodness of material things against "heretics" who show "lack of esteem for the flesh" (identified quickly by Montfaucon as manichees). Psalm 104.24 is cited in this defense, and extended commentary given to the opening verses of Ps 19 on the praise of God rendered by the heavens. The pesky Isaian verse has been allowed to drop out of sight until finally, with the preacher reaching the halfway mark, he admits to his having digressed, mentions the other readings, confesses to further difficulty in bypassing his beloved Paul, who "has often succeeded in making me lose my way," and professes to shaping up again to the prophetic verse which (he says) has disturbed some of the congregation.

Again, however, he refrains from his normal Antiochene style of close attention to details of the text in question, about the Lord's creating evils, and instead devotes the second half of the homily to philosophizing on the nature of things as neither good nor bad in every respect, but "in-between," morally indifferent. To document this approach he typically cites a range of scriptural examples – the afflicted Job, the affluent Abraham, the destitute Lazarus – after whom he moves to the fate of the Jewish people for whom captivity, servitude and exile proved to be blessings disguised as troubles. All of these are moral examples – platitudes, in fact – and eventually at the last gasp the preacher has to admit that the best he can do is to translate Isaiah into a similar platitude: "these things are weapons of virtue for those who use them properly;" they are neither good nor bad in every respect, but "in-between." And thus divine holiness and transcendence are preserved. Only once in all this skirting about the challenging text does Chrysostom concede that it must be seen for what it is, a paradox, not susceptible of reduction to moral truisms. That is when he finds in Amos (3.6) a similar paradox, "Is there any evil in the city for which the Lord was not responsible?" Very properly he advises his listeners to follow sound Antiochene hermeneutical principles: "Learn the force of these expressions." Had he from the outset adopted this principle, which he learned from Diodore of Tarsus,[3] he would have looked further in Isaiah for a clue to the paradox instead of trying to remove it.

Were one to have accepted editor Montfaucon's agnosticism as to place and date of this homily, the extended digressions employed – and the repetitive and meandering argumentation conducted within them – would have suggested a more advanced age than Chrysostom betrays in biblical commentaries we can associate with an earlier period of his ministry of the Word in Antioch. Coming as bishop (perhaps unprepared) to speak to a difficult text thrown up by the liturgy, on the other hand, he can perhaps be excused for trying to escape from its challenge, despite the quandary in which the congregation were left. We can still recognize in that day's second speaker the Chrysostom who commented earlier on the stories from the Former Prophets on Hannah and on David and Saul, on that Jeremiah verse 10.23, as well as on the complete text of Genesis and Psalms. The rationalizing applied to the Isaian paradox was found there, too, as was the ready documentation assembled from other parts of Scripture – frequently loosely recalled and applied, as here in the case of Job (like many a preacher, he adverts only to the protagonist of the book's prose framework, not the cursing plaintiff of the verse) and Ecclesiastes 3 (he recalls vv.2 and 4 in a form to suit his own theme, ignoring also the fatalism of the author). His Antiochene formation emerges in his insistence on the ἀκρίβεια of the text and its need in the commentator when he denies he is bypassing the Isaian verse "idly or to no purpose," and also in his urging his listeners to accept the παχύτης of the psalmist's reference to the heavens' praise of God while also warning the more materialistic (παχύτεροι) of them not to be misled by the text's anthropomorphisms.

An approach he might as commentator have helpfully brought to this problematic verse from Second Isaiah was to situate the verse in its wider context, were this possible for a bishop commenting perhaps *ex tempore* after noting the perplexity the passage gives rise to in the congregation, as he observes. A modern commentator with leisure to survey these chapters of the prophet would look at their overall structure, recognize their purpose in the commissioning of Cyrus, note the device of inclusion that links this verse 45.7 with 44.24, where similar key words are found – a hermeneutical procedure he recommended to those who misquoted Jer 10.23. A speaker arising on cue to allay his flock's concern, however, has not this leisure at his disposal, and so falls back on a tried stratagem like rationalizing and digression – a stratagem we appreciate the less after reading that homily on Jeremiah, which is such an impressive compendium of Antiochene hermeneutical principles patently not brought to bear on the Isaiah verse that day in Constantinople.

Homily on Isaiah 45.6-7

"I the Lord God brought light and darkness into being, making peace and creating evils" (Isa 45.6-7). [1]

While the words are few, they are a sweet source of honey, honey that brings no satiety. You see, whereas material honey leaves its sweetness on the tongue before being consumed and disappearing, the honey of instruction lies hidden in the conscience, providing constant good cheer and guiding us to incorruptibility; the former is collected from plants, the latter gathered from the divine Scriptures. With this the excellent speaker has given us our fill today, taking the responsorial verse as a trophy to give evidence of the force of love and the nobility of faith. Come, now, let us too spread before you in turn the customary banquet with great enthusiasm; after all, we are very pleased that, despite the glitter of the races, such a large number chose to turn away from spending time there to come here. [2] Hence let us on our part, too, offer the bowl with great liberality, a bowl that instead of causing drunkenness is productive of sobriety.

That, in fact, is what the wine of the Scriptures is like, that is what the viands of this banquet are like: you will not fall to flesh. Not that in saying this we are showing lack of esteem for the flesh: it is just that we give pride of place to nobility of soul, not to exclude indulgence but to curtail excess. Even if we practise sound values, you see, they must be practised in such a way as not to provide the mouths of heretics with a specious argument.[3] I mean, while this body of ours is inferior to the soul, it is not at odds with the soul; rather, though simple itself, yet it ministers to the body's desires. God the master craftsman, instead of forming the universe from one or two or three substances, brought forth many and varied natural things to give evidence of the abundance of his peculiar wisdom in the variety of things made: he created not only heaven but also earth, not only earth but also sun, not only sun but also moon, not only moon but also stars, not only stars but also sky, not only sky but also clouds, not only clouds but also upper air, not only upper air but also pools and springs and rivers, mountains and valleys and hills, meadows (143) and gardens, seeds and plants, many kinds of bushes, different appearances, different operations, different natures, which you could observe anywhere you went. Traversing in your mind the body of the world you would say with the inspired author, "How your works are magnified, O Lord! You made everything in wisdom."[4]

And so if it is a spectacle you are after, leave that satanic one and come to this spiritual one; if it is lyres you wish to listen to, ignore that awful ditty, tune up your mind to vibrancy, and reach a state of mental alertness and intellectual vigor. Note different sounds and distinct chords emitting a single harmonious melody from all quarters in honor of God the master craftsman, as if the wind's sound composed of different sounds produces a single note in praise of the creator, and strings make one impression on their own and a different one when in combination. For you to grasp the impression they make on their own, in your mind pluck heaven's string, and you will hear it emitting a loud sound and uttering praise to God. This, then, is what the inspired author also realised when he said, "The heavens recount God's glory, and the firmament proclaims the work of his hands."[5] Switch from that note to the note sounded by the day and the night, and you will observe these sounds emitting a sweeter melody than any lyre or harp, especially when someone understands how to pluck these chords. You ask, What sound do they make? Heaven has no mouth to open, no tongue, no palate, no teeth, no lips – so how is a sound formed? how does the day give voice? They are not instruments that produce a sound, in fact: day and night simply involve course of sun and moon and passage of time.

So in case any of the more materialistic people are upset or disturbed to hear this, listen to how the inspired author wrestles with the statement: having said, "The heavens recount God's glory," and "day upon day brings up a word, and night upon night reports knowledge," instead of stopping there he went on, "No speech, no words, no voices of theirs to be heard."[6] Now, what he means is something like this: day and night and heaven not only produce a sound, but it is clearer, more distinct and audible than human sounds. How and in what fashion? Listen to the statement itself: "No speech, no words, no voices of theirs to be heard." So what does that mean? It is a compliment to the sound they make, praise for their noise. I mean, my words are recognised by someone who speaks my language, but not by someone of a different tongue. For example, when I am conversing in the Greek language and someone knows that language, they will understand me, whereas the Scythian, the Thracian, the Moor, the Indian would not: the difference in language does not allow my meaning to become clear. (144) Likewise I will not succeed in understanding the Scythian or the Thracian when they are speaking, nor anyone else another person's language. But in the case of heaven and night and day this is not so: their voice is such as to be understood by people of every language, every speech, every nation, and to be meaningful and clear.

Hence after saying, "The heavens recount God's glory," and "Day upon day brings up a word," he went on, "No speech, no word, no voice of theirs to be heard." Now, what he means is something like this: day and night and heaven and all created things have such speech and such a sound as to be understood by all languages, that is, all tongues. There is no language, in fact – that is, no race, no voice – where heaven's voice will fail to be understood: the Scythian, the Thracian, the Moor, the Indian, the Sarmatian, every language and tongue and race will be capable of understanding this voice. How and in what fashion? Listen further so as to grasp how heaven gives voice without saying anything. You see, when you observed its beauty, its magnitude, its arrangement, its permanence, its splendor, and in pondering all these at once you gave glory to the creator, you praised the maker, it was then that heaven gave forth its voice, uttering glory to God with its tongue. This is the meaning of the verse, "The heavens recount God's glory." How and in what fashion? By directing the viewer to admiration of the creator by the beauty of it own brightness: when you see such a remarkable work, you say, Glory to you, O God, for creating such a mighty thing and setting it before our eyes; the heavens offered up this praise by using its own language and prompting admiration through sight of it. Though being silent in this way, they offer glory to God, and everyone understands their voice; it is possible to perceive it not by hearing but by sight and viewing, and sight is common to everyone even if languages are different and foreign, Scythians and Thracians and Moors and Indians understanding this voice, gazing at the marvel, struck by its beauty, its brightness, its magnitude and all the other aspects of the sky, offering praise to the creator if their attitude is sincere.

After all, when you observe the regularity of the times, and how day respects its own limits and is not at odds with night for the purpose of exceeding its own boundaries, nor displays any greed, nor exercises any pressure to use up all the time on the grounds of being brighter than night, but instead gives way, and night likewise on completing its course yields place to day; and how this has happened for all these years without any confusion or disturbance, and without one edging out the other or the latter begrudging the former, though one is brighter and the other darker – how would you not admire the regularity and offer glory to God? Like two sisters well disposed to each other, who divide up their patrimony with weights and balances without the one begrudging the other any slightest thing, (145) so too do night and day divide up the time between them and, without begrudging one another anything in the least, they preserve such equality as you know from experiencing it yourselves. Let the greedy take heed of this, who exclude their siblings from the inheritance; let them have regard for the regularity of the times, the equity of day and night, and let them put an end to this disorder of theirs. This, then, is the fashion in which "Day upon day brings up a word, and night upon night reports knowledge," not uttering a sound but through their regularity and rhythm, their equality and uninterrupted measure celebrating the creator more conspicuously than a trumpet, not in one corner of the world but in all the land the sun traverses. The voices themselves are carried everywhere in the world since the sky is everywhere, the day is everywhere, the night is everywhere, and they broadcast their teaching both on land and on sea. Hence the inspired author said not simply that the heavens utter the glory of God, but "recount"[7] – that is, instruct others, make disciples of the human race, and bring to the fore as the most convincing teaching in place of books and writing the beauty of their own nature and parade it for the notice of simple and learned and everybody, as though instruction in God's wisdom and power were lying in a book before them. This is not the manner of utterance of human beings: without saying a word they glorify God by other means – hence Christ's saying, "Let your light shine in people's sight so that they may see your good works and glorify your Father in heaven."[8] Just as you see an impressive life, then, and without a word from the one living it you offer glory to God, so too on seeing heaven's beauty you glorify the maker. Hence he said, "The heavens recount God's glory" by means of the eyewitnesses.

"Day upon day brings up a word, and night upon night reports knowledge." What sort of knowledge? About its maker: as day drives the human being out to work, so night comes in turn and brings rest from the countless concerns, gives relief from worries, brings sleep to tired eyes, closes the eyelids, and gets us ready to receive the sun's rays once again with renewed strength. And so its usefulness, far from being slight, is actually very considerable: if it did not give people rest by releasing them from countless worries, it would be no good for day to take them off to work, nature despairing under the ceaseless labor, and so the living being would be wasted and destroyed, and no benefit would come to them any longer from the sun's rays. By rendering the day useful for people, then, it leads them to the knowledge of God in particular by its peculiar ministry when they enjoy its dance. You see, when you understand the great usefulness of day and the great usefulness of night, and how one succeeds the other, and vice versa as though in a kind of dance, and by succeeding one another alternately they preserve the human race, you will be able by exercising your own powers of reasoning to recognise the wisdom of God the master-craftsman of which he gives evidence though the day and the night, allotting one to us for work and the other for rest from labors.

While we have digressed, however, to say all this from the beginning,[9] perhaps some of the things read to us today alarmed many who did not pay attention (146) and those not well versed in Scripture.[10] So, come now, let us move on to them with great diligence. There was also a reading, remember, about the woman with a flow of blood,[11] who with a touch put a stop to the blood-flow and by the power of faith purloined such a wonderful treasure. I mean, what happened was theft, but a praiseworthy theft at that, and the thief was due for commendation after being charged, Jesus himself though robbed celebrating that poor woman. There was also a reading about Paul's stripes, his wounds, his times in prison, his arraignments, his shipwrecks, his bonds, his chains, the manifold and unceasing attempts on his life, his dying daily, hunger, thirst, nakedness, rioting day in day out[12] – by why go on? I must keep a tight hold on myself and get off the subject in case Paul should once more get me in his clutches and lead me off the topic; often on other occasions, you recall, when I was up and running he has met me and laid hold of me in full flight, and succeeded in making me lose my way. So in case we have the same experience today as well, let us with great severity impose, as it were, a bridle on our discourse when it tends in that direction, and thus bring it around and make it bear on the inspired Old Testament verse.

What, then, is the verse? "I the Lord brought light and darkness into being, making peace and creating evils." Note that it was not idly or to no purpose[13] that we directed our steps to this spot: having bypassed all the other places we were anxious to arrive at this point. In the person not paying close attention, in fact, the verse instils deep concern. Attend carefully, therefore, sharpen your hearing, and by dismissing every worldly concern give heed to what is said. You see, I intend to give you this now by way of reward for being present here, and by filling you with the spiritual viands to send you off so that even those who absented themselves may learn by experience what loss they have sustained; they will know it if you take careful note of what is said and are in a position to pass it on to them. "I the Lord God brought light and darkness into being, making peace and creating evils." I keep going over it so that it will be engraved on your mind and then find a solution; he was not the only one to say this, a different author also being in agreement with him when saying, "Is there any evil in the city for which the Lord was not responsible?"[14] What is the meaning of this text? They all must have the one solution. So what is the solution? Learning the force of these expressions. But pay careful attention: it is not idly or to no purpose that we constantly make this recommendation to you, but because we are now proceeding to depth the meaning. Some things are good, others bad, others in-between; while some of them are thought bad by many people, in fact they are not, only being described and presumed to be.

For me to make clearer what I am saying, however, come now, let us reduce our point to its bare bones by examples as well. While by many people poverty is thought evil, in fact it is not; rather, if you look at it dispassionately and with sound values, it has the effect of removing evils. (147) While wealth likewise is thought by many people to be good, in fact it is not good in every sense if you do not use it properly. After all, if wealth were good in every sense, those possessing it would also be good; but if not all rich people are virtuous, only those using wealth well, obviously of itself wealth is not good, the substance of virtue as it were being in-between. Consider this: there are qualities in the body which give their name to people possessing them – for example, a fair complexion is not a substance but a quality, something which accidentally belongs to a substance, so if this affects a person, we call such a person fair. Likewise illness is also a quality accidentally occurring, and if it affects a person, we call such a person ill. So if wealth, too, were a virtue, it would follow that the person with wealth is and is said to be virtuous; but if the wealthy person were not at all virtuous, wealth is not in every sense virtue, nor is it good in every sense – rather, it becomes so, depending on the mindset of the one using it. Likewise, if poverty were evil, it would follow that all those living in poverty were evil, whereas if many of those living in poverty attained heaven, surely poverty is no evil.[15]

Why is it, then, you ask, that many people are driven by poverty to blaspheme? It is not by poverty: they do this out of their own lack of sense and mean-spiritedness. Blessed Job is proof of this: though in extreme poverty and brought to the very depths of poverty, far from blaspheming he kept blessing God in the words, "The Lord has given, the Lord has taken away, as the Lord pleased so did it happen: blessed be the name of the Lord forever."[16] But, you say, also on account of their wealth many people are rapacious and greedy. It is not on account of their wealth, however, but on account of their own lack of sense, this very man being witness likewise to this: though enjoying such great wealth he did not take what belonged to others, but even gave away what was his and prepared a haven for strangers, saying, "My house was open to every stranger who came."[17] Abraham, too, who had such great wealth, spent it all on passers-by. Wealth did not make the one or the other grasping, just as poverty did not cause Job or Lazarus to blaspheme; instead, though not being well-off for necessary nourishment, each was so conspicuous that one received testimony from God, who has a clear knowledge of unspoken thoughts, and the other was carried off from here by an escort of angels and made to dwell in the company of the patriarch and enjoy the same good things as he.

So these things are in-between – poverty and wealth, health and sickness, life and death, glory and honor, slavery and freedom, and suchlike. There is no need to go into them all, after all, lest the sermon become too lengthy, but only with these examples to provide you with the occasion of reaching on the more urgent issues; Scripture says, remember, "Give the wise an opportunity, and they will be wiser."[18] So all these things are in-between with the result that people can use them for good or for evil. Proof that they are in-between, including wealth, was given by Abraham, (148) who used it properly; also in the case of Lazarus the rich man also proved it, outlaying his possessions to the ruin of his own person. So wealth is not a good thing or a bad thing in all respects: if it were good in all respects and not in-between, the rich man in the case of Lazarus would not have suffered those awful punishments; if it were bad, Abraham with his riches would not have enjoyed such a good reputation.

Sickness is something similar: if sickness were bad, it would follow that the one with it would also be bad. Timothy, to be sure, would also have been destined to be bad on this score, struggling as he was with extreme sickness: "Take a little wine for your stomach's sake," Scripture says, "and on account of your frequent ailments."[19] But if it is not only true that he was not bad on that basis but actually received an additional reward in abundance through nobly bearing his infirmity, obviously sickness is not a bad thing. Another inspired author suffered from poor eyesight; but instead of being bad on that account, he was actually inspired and foresaw the future, sickness proving no obstacle to virtue.[20] Good health, on the other hand, is not good in all respects, either, unless one uses it properly and not for evil purposes or for mindless inactivity, which itself is not without fault; hence Paul also said, "If any are not prepared to work, let them not eat."[21]

These things are in-between, however, proving to be one thing in this circumstance, another in that, depending on the use we make of them. Why is it necessary to cite health and sickness, wealth and poverty? After all, not even the very things which in the estimation of the general run of people are the summit of good things or the height of bad – I mean death and life – are not so in all respects: they are in-between, proving one or other depending on the attitude of those who use them. To cite an example: living is good when someone uses it properly, but when used for sin and lawlessness, it is no longer good, and it would instead be better for such a person to pass on. Again, what in the estimation of the general run of people is to be avoided would be the source of countless goods when the cause of it is appropriate: witness the martyrs, who are more blessed than anyone on account of their passing. This was the reason Paul was not filled with longing in every respect to be alive in Christ – only since it was for him the fruit of work. "I am uncertain what to choose," he says, remember; "I am caught between the two, having the desire to be dissolved and be with Christ, this being far better; yet for your sake there is a more urgent need to remain in the flesh." [22] Hence the inspired author also said, "Honorable in the Lord's sight is the death of his holy ones" – not death in every respect but death of this kind – and again in another place, "Sinners' death is evil." [23]

Do you see that this is also one of the in-between things, not good in every respect nor bad in every respect, but depending on the attitude of those overtaken by it? This is the reason that the eminently wise Solomon, too, when listing the things of indifferent value and applying his reason to them, shows that one thing is not good in every respect or another bad, but they are rendered good in due season, even if they seem burdensome when the time is not ripe: "A time to weep and a time to laugh, a time to live and a time to die." [24] In other words, rejoicing is not always good: there are even times when it is harmful; (149) nor is grieving always good, there being times when it is fatal and ruinous. Paul likewise made this very point: "Grief as God would have it produces repentance leading to salvation and bringing no regrets, whereas grief in the world's fashion produces death."[25] Do you see that this, too, is one of the in-between things? Hence he did not bid us be joyful without qualification, but be joyful in the Lord.[26]

Our treatment has given you sufficient clarification of the in-between things, however. It is now time to proceed not to the in-between things but to the good things which could not be made bad and to the bad things that could not be made good. What were mentioned before, you see, are of one kind at one time, another kind at another time, such as wealth, which is bad at times when it is spent on greed, but good at times when it is consumed in almsgiving. And so with the other things of this kind according to this norm: there are some which at no time could be bad, and others, the opposite of these, which could at no time be good, like impiety, blasphemy, licentiousness, cruelty, inhumanity, gluttony and the like. I am not saying that a bad person could at no time become good, nor a good person at no time become bad: while those other things are in a class of their own, some good, some bad, the human being by contrast is good when opting for the former and bad when opting for the opposite.

There are, then, three categories of things: some good things could never be bad, like self-control, almsgiving and the like; some bad things could never be good, like licentiousness, inhumanity, cruelty; and some things become one or other at one time or another, depending on the attitude of the one who uses them. Wealth, for instance, sometimes contributes to avarice, sometimes to almsgiving, but depending on the attitude of the user. Poverty sometimes contributes to blasphemy, sometimes to blessing and resignation. Most irrational people, then (it is time to move to a conclusion), class as bad not only bad things that could never be good but also some in-between things as well, like poverty, captivity, servitude, which we have shown do not belong to bad things but to those that are in-between, whereas many people, as I said before, class as bad what are not really bad, of which the inspired author says they are not bad in reality though classed as such in the estimation of the general run of people, like captivity, servitude, hunger and suchlike.

You see, for proof that these things are not bad but even help to repel bad things, let us concentrate first on hunger, which everyone thinks is terrible and fearful. Get to know, then, how it is not bad, and learn to hold right values. When the Hebrew people were reduced to the extremes of lawlessness, then it was that the mighty Elijah, worthy of heaven, in his wish to overcome the ailment of indifference and correct it, kept on saying, "As the Lord lives before whom I stand, there will be no rain except by my word."[27] Though possessing only a mantle, he closed heaven, such confidence did he have in God. Do you see that poverty is not an evil? The most needy of men would not have enjoyed such confidence as to give evidence, while still walking this earth, of such marvelous power in a single word. By saying (150) this, then, he introduced hunger as an excellent pedagogue and reformer of incidental evils; and as when a raging fever strikes the body, torrents dried up along with plants, and the flanks of the earth from then on were infertile. Then it was that the people gained no little benefit by being rid of the flood of lawlessness, held in check, made more amenable, and rendered more responsive to the prophet; those who had taken themselves off to idols and sacrificed their children to the demons were the ones who had no objection to the slaughter of the priests of Baal, and instead of being upset they bore the event in silence and trepidation, made better by hunger.

Do you see that hunger is not only no evil but even acts to abolish evils, correcting ailments in the manner of a medicine? If you are prepared to see captivity also as no evil, consider what the Jews were like before the captivity, and what they were like during the captivity, so as to learn that neither is freedom good in all respects nor captivity bad. When they enjoyed freedom, remember, and had their own country, they committed such awful things that day in and day out the prophets railed against them for the laws being trampled underfoot, the idols worshiped, and God's commandments transgressed. But when they were taken off to a foreign land and lived in a country of savages, they were so chastened and turned into better people and observers of the Law that it is possible to grasp the fact from the psalm we are obliged to focus on today so as to learn the fruit of captivity. Which psalm is that? "By the rivers of Babylon there we sat and wept when we remembered Sion. On the willows in its midst we hung up our instruments. For there it was that the captors asked us to sing songs, saying, Sing for us some songs of Sion. How were we to sing the song of the Lord in a foreign land?" [28]

Do you see how captivity had chastened them? Before it, remember, they could not bear the prophets' ringing appeals not to break the Law, [29] whereas after it, despite pressure from the savages and their masters' urging and insisting, they did not respond, saying instead, We will not sing the Lord's song in a foreign land, since the Law does not allow it. Note also the three young men not only suffering no harm from captivity, but even rendered more conspicuous by it, and Daniel likewise. What of Joseph? what evil did he suffer, exile and slave and captive though he had become? did he not on that account only gain a good reputation and become famous? That foreign woman, living though she was in wealth and pomp and freedom – what good did she get from it? was she not the most wretched of all women for not being willing to put them to proper use?

These things have thus been clearly shown to you to be in some cases bad, some good and some in-between, and the fact that the inspired author is saying the in-between things are not really bad but thought to (151) be by the general run of people – captivity, servitude, exile. [30] Now, it is necessary to explain the reason for this statement. Loving as he is and quick to show mercy, while tardy in exercising retribution and punishment, God sent prophets so as to avoid consigning the Jews to punishment, intending to frighten them in word so as not to punish them in deed. He did this also in the case of the Ninevites: in that case he threatened to overthrow the city,[31] not with the intention of overthrowing it but to avoid overthrowing it, as in fact actually happened. This he did in this case as well, sending prophets, threatening the onset of savages, wars, captivities, servitude, exile, life in a foreign land. Just as a loving father with a recalcitrant and slothful child wishes to bring him to his senses and so goes looking for the whip and threatens the lash in the words, I shall tie you up, scourge you, do away with you, and he becomes fearsome in word so as in this way to subdue the young person's evil ways, so too God constantly threatened in his wish to make them better through fear. Observing this, and wishing to undermine the reform that was the result of such a threat, the devil sent down false prophets, and in contradiction of the prophets' threats of captivity, servitude and famine they preached the opposite – peace, prosperity and enjoyment of countless good things. Hence the prophets also mocked them by saying, "Peace, peace – and where is peace?"[32] This every scholar knows,[33] that everything happened as the prophets foretold against the false prophets, who were undermining the people's zeal.

So when they undermined the people in this way and corrupted them, God said through the prophets, "I God am making peace and creating evils." What sort of evils? Those mentioned – captivity, servitude and the like. Not fornication, licentiousness, avarice and anything else like that. Hence the other prophet in saying, "Is there any other trouble in the city for which the Lord was not responsible?"[34] refers to this trouble – famine, disease, plagues sent by God. Thus Christ also, in saying, "Sufficient for the day its own trouble,"[35] is referring to labor, effort, hardship. This, then, is what the prophet means: Do not let the false prophets undermine you; God can give you peace and consign you to captivity – the meaning of "making peace and creating evils." For you to learn that this is true, let us make a precise examination of the individual expressions: [36] after saying before, "I am the one who brought light and darkness into being," he then went on, "Making peace and creating evils." He cited two opposites first, and two opposites after that, for you to learn that he is referring not to fornication but to calamities. I mean, what is set as the opposite of peace? Clearly captivity, not licentiousness, nor fornication, nor avarice. So just as he cited two opposites first, so too (152) in this case; the opposite of peace is not fornication, nor adultery, nor licentiousness, nor the other vices, but captivity and servitude.

What their experience is of the elements, however, applies in these matters as well. For example, just as he made light and darkness, and most people think light is pleasant and darkness oppressive, and they misrepresent the night as something evil, so is it in these matters as well. Night, however, should not be misrepresented, nor darkness, nor should servitude in all respects, nor captivity. I mean, what is base, tell me, about darkness? is it not rest from labor? is it not relief from care? is it not removal of distress? is it not increase in strength? If there were no darkness and night, on the other hand, would we ever have enjoyed the light? would not this living thing that is the human being have been destroyed and lost? Now, just as foolish people think darkness is evil, and yet it is not, being instead of benefit to us and rendering those who have rested during it fitter for work, so too captivity is not worthless, either: the prophet was speaking of it when he said, "I make peace and create evils." On the contrary, it is of benefit to those who make proper use of it, rendering them more temperate and reasonable by removing their stupidity.

Virtue, you see, is not circumscribed, and nothing could prevail over it – not servitude, not captivity, not poverty, not disease, not what is more imperious than anything, death itself. This is clear from all those who endured all such things, and through them became more conspicuous: what harm came to Joseph (there is nothing to prevent our focussing on the same man again)? from his bonds? from his chains? from calumny? from scheming? from life in a foreign country? What harm came to Job from the loss of herds and flocks, the violent and untimely death of his children, bodily affliction, swarms of worms, unbearable pain, sitting on the dunghill, plotting by his wife, the taunts of friends, the abuse of servants? What harm came to Lazarus from lying in the gateway, from being licked by the tongues of dogs, from constant hunger, the rich man's contempt, the wounds, the unbearable disease, deprivation of patrons, contempt on the part of helpers? What harm came to Paul from the succession of those imprisonments, arrests, deaths, drownings and all the other trials which it is impossible to enumerate?

In considering all these things, let us shun evil, let us pursue virtue; and while we pray not to enter into temptation, let us, should we ever fall, not be distressed or upset. These things, you see, are weapons of virtue for those who use them properly,[37] and we shall succeed in gaining approval through them and enjoying eternal good things if we are alert. May it be the good fortune of us all to attain this in Christ Jesus our Lord, to whom be the glory for ages of ages. Amen.

CHRYSOSTOM'S SIX HOMILIES ON ISAIAH 6

While the previous homily on Isa 45.6-7, a text with which Chrysostom had to wrestle owing to its occurrence in a daily liturgy at which as bishop he preached, shows him struggling to render the prophet intelligible to his congregation, he nourishes a deep regard for "the most articulate of all the prophets." This esteem and the grounds for the accolade emerge clearly in the series of (five or) six homilies (known also by a Latin title *In Oziam*) on the opening verses of Isaiah 6 at the moment of the prophet's vocation, to which the preacher relates the incident in 2 Chr 26 of King Uzziah's thwarted attempt to arrogate to himself the role of high priest. Internal evidence suggests the short series was delivered in Antioch early in 387 immediately before Lent, and possibly in the wake of the two homilies on the obscurity of the Old Testament (which appear in our next volume). Questions about the number and order of these homilies we may leave till we have highlighted their exceptional features.

Although Chrysostom's customary moral approach to biblical texts is also here in evidence, what does distinguish the commentary are some beautiful formulations of Antiochene appreciation of the inspired Scriptures as a means of revelation and as an example of divine considerateness (συγκατά βασις) for human limitations (ἀσθένεια). Chrysostom reviews the divine considerateness demonstrated in the privilege accorded the seraphim and still more in the eucharistic κοινωνία with Christian communicants. Appreciating this loving gesture to seraphim and especially to human beings involves also, for an Antiochene, respecting limits proper to created natures. Chrysostom challenges in particular the kataphatic theology of the Anomeans, who wished to examine the un-examinable instead of accepting συγκατάβασις for what it is.

> This is the reason, at any rate, why they turn aside their faces and use their wings as a barrier, unable to bear the rays streaming from that source. And yet, you say, the vision was an example of considerateness (συγκατάβασις); so how was it they could not bear it? You ask me this? Ask those who pry into the ineffable and blessed nature, who presume where presumption is illicit. The seraphim would not succeed in seeing even this example of considerateness, whereas a human being would dare to claim – or, rather, manage to come up with the idea – that they are able precisely and clearly to see this nature for what it is. Tremble, O heaven! be aghast, O earth![1]

Uzziah serves to prefigure this anomean temerity, his arrogance being the true focus of the bulk of the preacher's attention in the homilies, and his leprosy fitting chastisement: "Such is the evil of not keeping to the limits of the gifts given us by God, whether this concerns office *or knowledge*," he adds, with a codicil of his own to The Chronicler's text.

From an exegetical point of view (using the term loosely to imply our principal interest), this continuing contrast between divine considerateness and seraphic awe, on the one hand, and on the other the temerity of Uzziah and the Anomeans has the effect of leading Chrysostom to express his own deep appreciation of scriptural κοινωνία. For him the biblical authors are the means by which communication (ὁμιλία) with God occurs, a communication which can be interrupted; and (with a loose application of the situation obtaining rather in the time of Eli as outlined in 1 Sam 3.1) he maintains that the people's unwillingness to expel the leprous Uzziah resulted in such an interruption of this scriptural communication.

Since they allowed him that liberty, therefore, God turned away from them and put a stop to the charism of inspiration (προφητεία) – and rightly so: in return for their breaking his law and being reluctant to expel the unclean one, he brought the charism of inspiration to a halt. "The word was precious at that time, and there was no inspired utterance," that is, God was not speaking through the inspired authors: the Spirit through whom they made utterance was not inspiring them since they kept the unclean one, the Spirit's grace not being active in the case of unclean people. Hence he kept his distance, he did not reveal himself to the inspired authors: he was silent and remained hidden... You refuse? I shall have no dealings with you, either.

This divine ὁμιλία, far from being merely functional and its interruption inconvenient, is of inestimable value; and while as a true Antiochene Chrysostom always maintains that the Scriptures can be subjected to scrutiny with precision, ἀκρίβεια, there are limits to be respected here, too.

The value of the Scriptures to the congregation (who are listeners to the word rather than readers of the text) is inestimable because of the divine inspiration of the authors; and the effect of this inspiration is the revelation it provides into the nature of the divine author and his purposes. The implication for the listener to this inspired and revealing word, then, is rapt attention: "The mouths of the inspired authors are the mouth of God, after all; such a mouth would say nothing idly – so let us not be idle in our listening, either." In Homily Two he dramatizes his listeners approach to the heavenly court in the company of Isaiah: "Pay precise attention, however: the reading out of the Scriptures is the opening of the heavens."[2] It is a theology of the Word with implications, of course, also for our age's liturgies: public reading of the lectionary is the congregation's key to heaven.

These six homilies, in short, are – to borrow a figure dear also to the preacher – a rich treasury of formulations of Antiochene esteem for the scriptural Word. They also provide an insight into the approach of that school to levels of meaning to be found in the sacred text. Though accepting from master Diodore an accent on the literal sense, Chrysostom's hermeneutics allow him to have recourse occasionally to a typological explanation of a text when Scripture itself encourages it: Hebrews gives him grounds in Homily One for seeing Joshua as a type of Christ leading us into a heavenly promised land. But even his congregation resists an essay into allegory; on the subject of the devil's arrogance he has to forego any support from another Isaian text (14.14, the words rather of the king of Babylon) and settle for Paul's plain statement to Timothy (1 Tim 3.6):

> If, on the one hand, we cite Isaiah as witness in his words about him, "I shall rise up to heaven, and I shall be like the most high," those not happy to accept allegories will reject our testimony; if, on the other hand, we call Paul to prosecute him, no one will have any further objections.

He knows, on the other hand, that his Antioch congregation will have no problems with an exercise in θεωρία once the literal sense of his text has been commented on, as in the "mystical" interpretation he gives to the seraphs' covering their faces and feet with their wings.

Chrysostom characteristically adopts a moral stance in these homilies; he does not spend long on the dogmatic content of Isaiah's vision and vocation, except perhaps on Homily Six, preferring to adopt a moral approach to Uzziah's sin and its punishment. Though at one point he declares that the inspired text is all about historical detail ("It is, in fact, what proves prophecies to be prophecy: prophecy is nothing else than the prediction of future events. How, then, will the person ignorant of the mention of events and outcomes be able to prove to the adversary the worth of the prophecy?"), the particular focus of his study of Uzziah is the capital sin involved, ῥᾳθυμία, indifference, the cause of the Fall. In Homily Two he also adverts to the parable of the talents (Matt 25.14-30), from which the appropriate lesson for an

Antiochene is that we must all make our own contribution if we are to win God's favor: "What is looked for by God even among human beings, you see, is not whether we come up with little or much, but making an offering that is in no way less than the ability we have."

In conclusion: without perhaps being aware of similar misgivings of commentators from the seventeenth century onwards, the reader of these homilies notes some inconsistency in movement of thought. As we observed above, they deal not simply with Isaiah 6, of which only the opening verses come in for treatment, but predominantly with the story in 2 Ch 26 of King Uzziah's punishment for his effrontery in daring to assume the role of high priest. The inconsistencies are as follows. The local bishop is mentioned as being present for Homilies Two and Three; he is not referred to in Homily One, which does not contain material to which Homily Two refers when it says,

> The other day, when we had the honor of speaking to your good selves, you heard that psalm read out that expelled the sinner from the sacred precincts and bade angels and the powers on high praise the God of all.

At the end of Homily Six the preacher sums up for his congregation, but makes no attempt to include the material covered in the other homilies, even though earlier on that occasion he implies that the one congregation has been with him throughout:

> I have been noticing everyone hankering after the seraphim, not today only, but also from the first day.

Also in Homily Six the preacher refers to the approach of Lent, whereas in Homily Four conditions are said to be uncomfortably summery:

> Yesterday, remember, we wondered why on earth it is that, when all the inspired authors including this one customarily mention the time of the king's life, there is here a departure from the custom: he speaks not of the lifetime of Uzziah but

of the death of Uzziah. I intend to solve this today. Even if the temperature is high, you see, the dew from the sermon is greater; even if the body that is pampered finds the going heavy, the soul that is vigorous is exhilarated. Do not speak to me of heat and sweat: if your body is sweating, sponge your mind.

Furthermore, that accent on King Uzziah's death had in fact not been raised by the preacher in Homily Three (to cite the numbers of the homilies as they stand today without settling those early doubts about order of delivery).

The issues concerning number, order and even authenticity of the homilies are debated in endnotes. Suffice it to say that, following a thorough search of the wider Chrysostomic corpus, reason can be found at least for retaining all six in the collection, if not proving a series in their present order. Chrysostom is clearly among the lower clergy and therefore ministering in Antioch in delivering at least some of the homilies; a date of early 387 for all but Homily One recommends itself. With judgement suspended on such paleographical and historical issues, the reader is justified in simply appreciating the theological riches of a text taken at face value and the preacher's skill as a biblical commentator on this "most articulate of all the prophets."

Homily One
Of those attending church, and on orderliness in the divine praises.
And on the verse, "I saw the Lord seated on a lofty and exalted throne." [1]

I see the evidence you give of great zeal for putting into effect what was said to you the other day.[2] That is the reason why I for my part spare no effort in sowing the seed, therefore, buoyed up as I am by sound hope. The farmer, too, after all, when he takes pains to sow the seed, has in view the land's fertility and the crops' abundance, and he forgets the recent labors, prompted to continuing effort and preservation by the prospect of gain.[3] And yet how much more prosperous and gainful does this cultivation prove to be! While that kind bears an abundance of material produce and contributes to bodily nourishment, this kind sows instruction by word, and in its copious supply of gifts of the Spirit it lays up wealth for the soul, nourishment that is inexhaustible and untainted, that does not run short or become spoilt with the passage of time but is preserved by some ineffable providence, possessing as it does a spiritual enjoyment. This is the yield of my labors, this the wealth contributed by your love.

When I reflect on this growth in you, therefore, I rejoice constantly that it is not in vain that I sow the seed, that it was not in vain that I underwent my labors, that I cultivated prosperous and fertile soil likely to bear a rich harvest. On what basis, then, do I count on such gain? on what basis do I get the impression of my words taking effect? Obviously from the present assembly, from your zealously occupying this the mother of the churches, from your being here all night without interruption, from your imitating the angelic choir in offering constant hymn-singing to the Creator.[4] How wonderful the gifts of Christ! On high hosts of angels sing praise, on earth in serried ranks in churches human beings in imitation of them sing the same praises. On high the seraphim raise the threefold hymn, here-below the multitude of human beings offer up the same hymn, a joint celebration performed by heavenly and earthly beings – one thanksgiving, one exultation, one chorus of joy. The Lord's ineffable considerateness,[5] you see, achieved this combination, the Holy Spirit fused it together, its harmony of voices was woven by the Father's benevolence; from on high comes the rhythm of its melodies, (98) and plucked by the Trinity like a kind of plectrum it gives off a sweet and blessed air, the angelic strain, the unending symphony.

This is the outcome of the enthusiasm shown here, this the fruit of our assembling. Hence my joy at seeing such deep satisfaction, my joy at grasping the happiness in your souls, the spiritual elation, the godly exuberance. Nothing, in fact, renders our life so joyous as the satisfaction felt in church: in church the joy of those rejoicing is maintained, in church there is encouragement for the discouraged, in church happiness for the grief-stricken, in church relief for the overburdened, in church respite for the exhausted. "Come to me," Scripture says, remember, "all who labor and are heavily burdened, and I shall give you rest."[6] What could be more appealing than this statement? what sweeter than this invitation? By inviting you in church the Lord invites you to good cheer, he urges you to rest in place of labor, he brings you to repose in place of pain, lightening the weight of sin; delights heal depression, happiness heals grief.

O what remarkable care on his part, what a heavenly invitation! Let us hasten, then, dearly beloved, to give evidence of the same heightened enthusiasm, and bring it to perfection with due orderliness and proper concentration. Today, in fact, my intention is to direct my words to you on this topic, words which may seem to be sobering but which in truth are inoffensive and beneficial. It is what loving parents do, after all: they give their children lessons not only of the kind that are entertaining in the short term but also those that vex them, they offer them advice not only of the kind that is obviously to their benefit but also what, while seeming to be burdensome, is salutary when performed; this is the instruction they give with great care, and they are insistent in requiring its observance. We make this point at length in case the effort we expend here be in vain, in case while forced to keep late hours we flay about aimlessly, in case our voice disappears into thin air and sounds off to your loss rather than your gain. To take the example also of a merchant who despatches cargo to foreign parts, and risks the fierce onslaught of winds and big waves: (99) it is not idly or to no purpose that he takes on the experience of such labors; instead, he plies the seas, exposes himself to risk, moves from place to place, and experiences completely sleepless nights for this purpose, to increase the value of his merchandise. If this by chance were not to happen, and instead he sustained loss of capital along with profit, it would not be worth his while to go to sea or undergo those manifold perils.

Aware of this, then, let us attend here with due piety lest we incur an increase in sin instead of their forgiveness, and so make our way home. Now, what is the question and the response required of us? That we raise the divine hymns chastened by deep fear and adorned with piety, and in this fashion offer them up. You see, there are some people present – unbeknown to you, I believe, dearly beloved – who with no respect for God treat the sayings of the Spirit as nothing special, and give vent to disorderly voices and conduct themselves no better than lunatics, cavorting and shaking their whole bodies, giving evidence of behaviour inconsistent with a spiritual condition. Poor wretch that you are, you should utter the angelic praises in fear and trembling, make confession to the Creator with dread, and thus beg pardon for your faults; instead, in this place you introduce the manners of actors and dancers, waving your hands about in disorderly fashion, kicking up your heels, and tossing your whole body about. How is it you are not fearful and terrified in the face of such sayings? do you not understand that the Lord is present here invisibly, scrutinising each person's behavior and examining their conscience? do you not understand that angels serve this awesome table and attend it in fear? You do not grasp this, however, since your mind is dulled with the sounds and sights of the spectacles, and that is the reason you mix what goes on there with the church's rituals, that is the reason you bring out into the open the disorder of your soul with mindless shouting.[7]

How, then, will you beg pardon for your sins?[8] how will you win the Lord over to mercy if you conduct your appeal with such scant respect? "Have mercy on me, O God," you say, and then give evidence of behaviour at variance with mercy; "save me," you cry, and then exemplify a deportment inconsistent with saving. Why do they raise their hands on high in supplication with constant gesturing and disordered cavorting, and why the loud meaningless cries accompanied with expulsion of breath? Are these not the manners of strumpets plying their trade in alleyways, in one case, and in the other the behavior of those sounding off at the spectacles? So how dare you mix demons' tricks with these angelic rites of praise? have you no respect for the verse you utter, "Serve the Lord in (100) fear, and in trembling rejoice in him"?[9] Does serving him in fear mean being scattered and dissipated, not even knowing what you are talking about in the disordered outpouring of your voice? This is a mark of disrespect, not fear, of arrogance, not humility; this is characteristic rather of those who jest than those who sing praise.

So what is the meaning of serving the Lord in fear? Discharging all his commands and doing so in fear and humility, offering supplication with contrite heart and humbled attitude. And the Holy Spirit through the inspired author bids us not only serve in fear but also rejoice in trembling. Since, you see, the discharge of the commandments normally imparts joy to the one practising virtue, it is proper for us to do so (the text says) with trembling and awe lest we be undone by our lack of fear, forfeit the benefit of our labors and provoke God. Now, how does it come about, does the text say, that we rejoice in trembling? After all, it is not possible for the two to happen together, there being considerable difference between them: joy is fulfilment of desire, enjoyment of pleasure, forgetting unpleasant things, whereas fear is a heightening of evils expected, pitted against a guilty conscience. So how is it possible to rejoice in fear, and not simply in fear but in trembling, which is a heightening of fear and a sign of great anguish? How, does the text tell us, will this occur?

The seraphim themselves will instruct you in practice by discharging such a ministry, enjoying as they do the ineffable glory of the Creator and contemplating his unimaginable beauty. I am not referring to it as it is by nature (it cannot be comprehended, after all, cannot be looked upon, cannot be imagined, and speculating in this way about it is wrong),[10] but to the extent granted them, to the extent that they are able to grasp it in the light of that ray. Since they are in constant attendance around the royal throne, you see, they live in constant joy, in eternal happiness, in unceasing elation, rejoicing, exulting, singing praise without let up. To stand in the presence of the glory, after all, and be enlightened by the brilliance beaming from it – this is their joy, this their elation, this their happiness, this their glory.

Perhaps you have had some experience of delight, and have had a longing for that glory. If, however, you are prepared to heed his exhortation and perform the present worship with reverence, you will not be deprived of this joy, since it is the Lord himself exhorting, who is given glory in heaven and on earth. Scripture says, remember, "Heaven and earth are full of his glory."[11] So how is it that those beings who enjoy such happiness mix fear with it? Listen to what the prophet says: "I saw the Lord seated on a lofty and exalted throne." Why did he first say "lofty" and then add "exalted"?[12] was it not sufficient to indicate the totality by the word "lofty" and show the pre-eminence of the dignity? (101) So what reason did he have in adding "exalted"? To bring out the incomprehensible character of the seat. I mean, the word "lofty" gives us some understanding of a comparison with earthly and lowly things; for example, mountains are lofty compared with plains and rifts in the earth, the sky is lofty in being lifted up over all earthly things. But it is the exaltation and eminence of that incomprehensible nature alone which is impossible to conceive or comment on – hence the saying, "I saw the Lord seated on a lofty and exalted throne."

And what else did you see, O prophet? what did you espy around about him? "The seraphim were in attendance around him,"[13] the text says. Doing what, and saying what? showing what degree of boldness? No boldness, it says; instead, full of fear and astonishment, and in their demeanor showing the ineffable degree of their dread: with two of their wings they covered their faces, blocking the ray proceeding from the throne through their inability to cope with its unbearable glory, and at the same time also betraying the peculiar reverence which they have for the Lord. They rejoice with such great joy, they exult with such great happiness, and cover not only their faces but also their feet. Why do they do that? I mean, it is right for them to cover their countenance on account of the awesome nature of the vision and their inability to gaze at the unapproachable glory – but why do they conceal their feet? I meant to leave this to you to encourage you to work at an answer to it yourselves and to prompt you to study of spiritual things; but in case I leave your minds to be caught up in this puzzle and am the cause of your missing out on the exhortation, I had better let you off the hook. So why do they cover their feet? They are anxious to display untiring reverence for the Creator, a great effort that emerges in their deportment, their voice, their appearance and their very stance. Since they fall short of what is desirable and what is proper, they conceal the omission by covering everything up in all parts.[14]

Did you grasp what I said, or should I go over it again? For it to become clearer, however, I shall try to make it obvious from examples on our part. Someone attends on an earthly king, makes every effort to give evidence of deep reverence for him so as to win greater favor from him by this means. To this end, by the position of the head, the voice, the clasping of the hands, the joining of the feet and the total bodily deportment they make such reverence their object.[15] This happens with those incorporeal powers as well: with their earnest desire for reverence to the Creator, they take every means to display it, and when they fall short of their aim, (102) they put a covering over what does not match their desire. This is the reason, therefore, that they are said to cover their faces and their feet – though there is another more mystical interpretation to be given to this:[16] it is not that they have feet and faces (being incorporeal, as is also the divinity), but that by these means language may express that they are abased, and in fear and reverence they minister to the Lord.

This is the way we, too, should attend on him, offering similar praise-giving to him, in fear and trembling, as though having his very person in the eyes of our mind. There is present here, after all, the one who is completely uncircumscribed and who registers the cries of everyone. So let us likewise offer up prayer with contrite and humbled heart, and thus render it acceptable and offer it up to heaven like fragrant incense. "A contrite and humbled heart," Scripture says, remember, "God will not despise."[17] But the inspired author, you object, exhorts us to do our praise-giving with exultation: "Exult in the Lord, all the earth."[18] It is not such exultation, however, that we forbid, but mindless noise; not the sound of petition but the sound of disorder, wrangling with one another, hands raised in the air idly and to no purpose, kicking up the heels, the unbecoming and dissipated behaviour that amuses the people who spend their time at the spectacles and race track. It is from that source that these baleful notions are introduced in our midst, from that source come these impious and vulgar cries, from there the disorderly hand movements, the fights, the wrangles, the disorderly habits.

Nothing, in fact, is so calculated to bring contempt on God's sayings as people carried away with what was seen in those places. Hence my frequent urging anyone attending here, profiting from the divine instruction and participating in the awesome and mystical sacrifice,[19] not to betake themselves to those awful shows and mingle the divine sacraments with the demonic rites. Yet some people are so crazed that despite the pious demeanor they display and the advanced old age they have attained they still head off to those rites, neither heeding our words nor ashamed of the figure they cut. Instead, when we labor the point with them and urge them to show some respect for their grey hair and the solemnity of the occasion, how paltry and ridiculous their response! It is a harbinger of future victory and coronation, they claim, and we reap exceptional benefit from it. What are you saying, mortal that you are? This a well-worn reply, riddled with error. From what source do you reap benefit? from those countless wrangles and the oaths tossed about idly and to no purpose to the detriment of the speakers? or from the abusive, slanderous and scurrilous remarks that the observers of this behavior pour out on one another? But if it does not come from this, do you gather a beneficial effect from the utterly disorderly cries, mindless shouting, clouds of dust, people pushing and shoving and trying to make an impression on women? In this place, in fact, all the inspired authors and teachers give a glimpse of the Lord of angels seated on a lofty and exalted throne, awarding prizes and crowns to the deserving, and assigning hell and fire to the undeserving; (103) the Lord himself confirms it.[20] And so do you, on the one hand, despise things that involve a fear-stricken conscience, rendering an account of actions, struggling to justify conduct, and impartial verdicts, and on the other hand for the sake of coming up with an irrational excuse for your thrills you claim to derive benefit from the incorrigible loss you sustain? Do not, I beg and implore you, do not feign excuse in your sin: it is pretence and deceit, by which we bring trouble on ourselves.

So much for that, however; now is the time to return to our former exhortation and, after saying little about it, to bring our treatment to a fitting conclusion. You see, the trouble here is not only the matter of disorderly behavior: some other worse ailment also is afoot. What in fact is it? To set about entering into converse with God and offer up praise to him, then to ignore him and each one take up with his neighbor and arrange affairs at home, in public, in community, at the spectacles, in the army, how some matters are attended to and others neglected, which things are prospering in business and which failing – in short, conduct a discussion in this place about every matter personal and communal. What excuse would this deserve? If, for example, someone were conversing with the earthly emperor and keeping to the subject in which he was interested and to which he directed his enquires, and then if the person presumed to introduce some other matter at variance with his intentions, he would be liable to the extreme penalty. In your case, by contrast, if you were in intimate dialogue with the king of kings, to whom angels minister in awe, would you ignore the converse with him and speak of dirt and dust and spiders? This, in fact, is what is happening at present. How will you bear the penalty for contempt? who will deliver you from such awful punishment?

But, you object, business is doing badly and the country doing badly, and there is much to be said on the subject by us, much trouble to take. Whose fault is that? The stupidity of rulers, you reply. It is not the stupidity of rulers, but our sin, the dues payable for our faults. This is what turned things upside down, this is the source of all those problems, this is what brought on the wars, this is what caused our defeat; the swarm of disasters emerged from no other source than this cause.[21] And so even had an Abraham been in power, a

Moses, a David, a Solomon in all his great wisdom, even a person more sinful than anyone,[22] they would have made no difference to the problems. How on earth is that the case? Because if they were amongst the most lawless, amongst those who acted stupidly and in disorderly fashion, such people were the fruit of our stupidity and our disorder, it was our sins that brought on the calamity. In other words, our getting rulers in keeping with our own hearts means nothing other than this, that for our sins we had the bad luck to get a governor of this kind, be he one of the clergy,[23] be he one of the civil administrators. (104)

Had he even been exceedingly righteous, however, even so righteous as to match the virtue of Moses, his righteousness alone would not have succeeded in cloaking the excessive failings of his subjects. You could get a precise grasp of this from Moses himself: though he suffered many tribulations on behalf of Israel, and raised many entreaties to God for them that he might give them the promised land as an inheritance, yet since by their own sins they rendered themselves ineligible for the promise, his prayer was not able to alter God's just verdict on the whole people's being laid low in the desert. And yet who could be more righteous than Moses? or who enjoyed greater confidence with God? The prayer of a righteous person is said to prevail, but it is made efficacious[24] – that is, assisted – by the repentance and conversion of those for whom it is offered. In the case of those whose behavior is unrepentant and unconverted, on the other hand, how will it succeed in helping them while they themselves obstruct it by their actions? Why mention this happening in the case of the whole people's transgression when even the sin of a few subjects, or in many cases even one, proved too much for the influence of just rulers? You could come to realise this in turn from Israel itself: under Moses' governance they made incursions against the land of foreigners and waged war against them; when some of them lost their heads over those people's women, they brought on the whole community that awful ruin and destruction.[25]

This is the kind of thing that happened in the case of one person: Achan, for example, exempted the multi-colored robe from the ban and enkindled God's wrath against the people. Perhaps, however, some of those present are unfamiliar with this story; hence there is need to say a little about it to remind those who know it and instruct those who do not.[26] This man Achan, as it happens, was one of those who crossed the Jordan with Joshua son of Nun, who had been chosen by God's decision as Moses' successor, and who represented an image and type of our real Savior Jesus Christ: just as he conducted the people out of the desert across the Jordan into the promised land, so too our Savior transferred us from the desert of ignorance and idolatry through holy and saving baptism to the Jerusalem on high, to the mother of the firstborn, in which are prepared the abodes of true rest, where existence is peaceful and free from uproar.[27] This man, then, led the people across with the power of the one who directed them, assaulted Jericho, and put into effect that novel siege. When the walls were ready to fall down, what did he say to the people? "This city and all that is in it will be under a ban to the Lord of hosts except for Rahab the prostitute: spare her. So observe the ban, never tempted to take anything from it and destroy us."[28] Everything in the city, he means, is consecrated (which is what the ban implies); so no one is to appropriate anything devoted to the Lord God, or (105) they will be the means of our expulsion from the land.

Observance of the commandment was critical, involving great precision on the part of God in imposing it and Joshua as legislating for it. After all, in such a large body of people how could this law fail to be transgressed, with so many factors driving them to it? That is to say, the mob's instability and desire for gain, or the fact that not everyone was responsive to the imposition of the commandment, or the variety of spoils set before them like a bait to tempt those who were acquisitive would easily have driven them to transgression. Yet this law had been imposed, and the risk of transgression hung over their head. So what followed this? The walls came down, and everything in the city fell into the hands of those conducting the siege. Accordingly, though the whole people observed this commandment, the transgression by one person brought God's wrath on the whole multitude. "The children of Israel," the text says, remember, "committed a great fault, appropriating and taking from the ban: Achan son of Carmi took from the ban, and the Lord's wrath was aroused against the children of Israel."[29] Actually, the failure was on the part of one person; so how did the children of Israel commit it and the Lord's wrath become aroused against the children of Israel? Do you see how the sin of one person was the cause of retribution for the whole people? how it made God hostile to the multitude? Since, then, the offence had been committed, and no one was aware except the God who knows secrets, retribution was due, and the one who had done it, though seeming to have gone undetected, was scorched by conscience as though by fire. So the time came for the threat to be implemented and the sin to be made obvious. "Joshua sent men from Jericho to Ai," the text goes on. "About three thousand men went up there, and they fled before the men of Ai, who killed thirty six men of their number, pursued them, and crushed them. The heart of the people was dismayed and turned to water."[30]

Note the account exacted for one sin, note the irremediable affliction: one person sinned, and on the whole group fell death and terror. Why so, O good Lord? You alone are righteous, and your judgements sure. You impose your judgements on everyone according to their actions. You said, lover of humankind, that everyone dies in their own sin, and will not be punished for someone else's.[31] So what kind of just sentence of yours is this? All your doings are upright, Lord, indeed very upright, and arranged for our advantage. Sin is a kind of injury, he replies; to avoid everyone being injured, therefore, let it be bruited abroad through the punishment with a view to their knowing the awful threat posed by one transgression and avoiding the unending chastisement coming from many. Seeing the desperate flight, the text goes on, Joshua tore his garments and fell to the ground, giving vent to those awful laments which the divine Scripture reports. So what did the Lord say to him? "Get up: why are you flat on your face like this? Your people sinned and transgressed my covenant, and (106) the children of Israel will be unable to stand and face their enemies until you remove the consecrated things from your midst."[32] This was proclaimed in the midst of the people, and the one guilty of the transgression was denounced by God; the fellow concurred, the text says, Achan replying to Joshua in these words, "It is true I sinned before the Lord God of Israel. I did such and such: I saw amongst the booty a simple robe, of many colors and very beautiful, two hundred didrachmas of silver and a bar of gold worth fifty didrachmas; I took a fancy to them and stole them – see, they are all hidden in the ground in my tent."[33] Then he brought everything into the open on seeing that the one denouncing him was above falsehood and he had a factual witness to prosecute him. Note his ignominious and awful death: "Joshua took him up to the valley of Achor with his sons, his daughters, his calves, his beasts of burden, his sheep, his tent and all his possessions, and all Israel stoned them."[34] This was the recompense for lawlessness, this was the manner of God's incorruptible justice.

Aware of this, then, let us consider the troubles to be the outcome of our own guilty actions, and daily examine our faults, so as to attribute responsibility not to others but to our very selves. It was not only, in fact, the rulers' negligence but much more our failings that brought on the problems. In this way, then, let each person attending here consider their own faults and not blame anyone else, but with due decorum offer up the praise-giving happening here.[35] Now, the decorum required of us is as follows: firstly, to approach God with contrite heart, then also to display the disposition of heart in our visible demeanor, in our posture, in the orderly motions of our hands, in a gentle and moderated voice; this is easy and within the power of anyone so inclined. How, then, will the observance affect everyone? Let us make it a law for ourselves and say that a commandment has been imposed for general utility and that all should share in the benefit. For this reason let us suppress disorderly cries and keep under control the movement of our hands, presenting them joined together before God and not lifting them up in unbecoming motions – something God hates and abhors, just as he loves and welcomes the person of restraint: "On whom shall I look favorably," he says, remember, "if not the gentle and peaceable person who trembles at my words?"[36] Let us say to one another that he does not want us to speak with him and converse with one another, nor abandon speaking with him to get involved in the fortunes of those present, and soil pearls with mire; he takes this kind of thing as a personal insult, not praise-giving.

And should someone be intent on breaking this commandment, let us stop their mouth as we would expel someone plotting against our salvation, and drive them from the precincts of the holy church; by doing this we shall easily wash away former sins, on the one hand, and on the other have the Lord himself (107) in our midst, joining in the chorus of the holy angels and presenting each of us with the award for orderliness. Since he is loving and bountiful, you see, and rejoices in our salvation, hence with delight in our good deeds he promised the kingdom of heaven and a share in incorruptible life, and he prepared every good thing in his wish for us to dwell amongst them. May it be the good fortune of us all to attain this, thanks to the grace and lovingkindness of our Lord Jesus Christ, to whom belongs glory, power, honor and adoration with the Father and the Holy Spirit, now and forever, for ages of ages. Amen.[37]

Homily Two
On the inspired verse, "In the year that king Uzziah died I saw the Lord seated on a lofty and exalted throne."[1]
And the fact that time or any other item of the Divine Scriptures should not be passed over.

I rejoice to see you come running to hear the divine sayings, and I take it as the clearest sign of your advance in godliness: just as being hungry is a sign of the body's wellbeing, so the longing for spiritual discourse is a sign of the soul's health. While I rejoice on that account, then, I am afraid I may never provide anything worthy of that longing. In somewhat similar fashion, too, a loving mother is distressed when she has a child at the breast but is unable to provide it with an abundant flow of milk; yet despite being found wanting she still offers the breast, and the child takes it, and pulls and stretches it, and by warming the cooled nipple with its mouth it entices more than there really is. Though the mother feels sore with the stretching of the breasts, she does not push the child away: being a mother she would prefer to put up with anything rather than upset the baby.[2]

If, then, mothers are so affectionate towards their offspring, much more should this be our disposition towards your good selves, the pangs of spiritual birth being more ardent than those of natural birth. And so even if our table bears all the signs of great poverty, instead of concealing what there is we shall set before you all we have to offer; and even if it is paltry scraps, we shall offer it nonetheless. For that fellow who was entrusted with the talent was not called to account because he did not produce five talents; rather, he paid the penalty because he actually put in the ground what he had received.³ What is looked for by God even among human beings, you see, is not whether we come up with little or much, but making an offering that is in no way less than the ability we have.

The other day, when we had the honor of speaking to your good selves, you heard that psalm read out that expelled the sinner from the sacred precincts and bade angels and the powers on high praise the God of all.⁴ Do you want us today as well to listen to the mystical song, (108) taking our position close by them in some fashion? I am inclined to think so, anyhow. After all, if depraved people take a position in the market place at the dead of night, and by singing filthy ditties and dissolute songs they excite the whole city and bring them out to join them, shall we not hasten to listen to that divine and blessed sound when the heavenly ranks, the choirs on high, celebrate the king of this whole world? What excuse would we have?

How, you ask, can we listen to them? By mounting to heaven itself, if possible, if not actually in body, at least in intention; if not actually in presence, at least in mind. The body, after all, is earthly and heavy, and naturally stays herebelow, whereas the soul is free of this necessity and boldly takes wing to the most lofty and distant places, so that even if it wishes to go to the very ends of the earth and ascend to heaven, there is nothing to prevent it, so light the wings of thought God has given it. Not only has God given it light wings: he has also bestowed eyes that have much keener sight than the body's. The body's sight, after all, is carried through empty space and travels for a long distance; but if it strikes a small object, it is blocked and comes backwards.⁵ The eyes of the soul, by contrast, even if they encounter walls, ramparts, the magnitude of mountains, even the heavenly bodies themselves on the way, will pass them by easily.

The soul nevertheless, though having speed and keenness

of this kind, is not sufficient of itself for grasping heavenly realities: it needs the one who guides it. So let us do what is done by those who long to see the royal courts. What in fact do those people do? After searching for the keeper of the door keys, they approach him, speak to him and make a request, and often pay him money for granting them a favor. So let us, too, make our approach to one of the heavenly door keepers, speak and make a request, and in place of money give evidence of a sincere attitude and intention. And if that person accepts the payment, he will take us by the hand and conduct us everywhere, showing not the kingly apartments as such but the king himself enthroned, attended by hosts under the command of generals, myriads of angels, thousands of archangels; he will give us a precise glimpse of everything to the extent it is possible for us to see.[6] Who is it, then? who is entrusted with this role by which we now wish to make an entry? Isaiah, the most articulate of the inspired authors. So we must speak with him.

Let us follow him, however, with measured gait, moving in complete silence. Let no one enter burdened with worldly concerns, no one wavering, no one in the grip of passion; instead, let us leave all these things outside the doors, and all of us (109) enter in this fashion. It is the kingdom of heaven we are entering, after all, we are going to places where lightning flashes. Inside it is all silence and mysteries beyond telling. Pay precise attention, however: the reading out of the Scriptures is the opening of the heavens.[7] "In the year that King Uzziah died," he says, "I saw the Lord seated on a lofty and exalted throne." Do you see the friendly attitude of a thoughtful servant? He immediately brought us into the royal throne without first conducting us through long entrances; rather, he opened the doors and at the same time showed the king seated directly in front of us. "The seraphim had taken their position around him," he goes on, "each with six wings: with two they covered their faces, with two their feet, and with two they were flying. Each cried out to the other, saying, 'Holy, holy, holy, Lord of hosts.'" [8]

Truly holy for vouchsafing our nature so many and such wonderful mysteries, for making us sharers in such things beyond telling. Fear and trembling took possession of me in the midst of this recital. Small wonder if I, who am from mire and soil, am so affected when in fact the deepest stupor always grips even the very powers above. This is the reason, at any rate, why they turn aside their faces and use their wings as a barrier, unable to bear the rays streaming from that source. And yet, you say, the vision was an example of considerateness;[9] so how was it they could not bear it? You ask me this? Ask those who pry into the ineffable and blessed nature, who presume where presumption is illicit. The seraphim would not succeed in seeing even this example of considerateness, whereas a human being would dare to claim – or, rather, manage to come up with the idea – that they are able precisely and clearly to see this nature for what it is.[10] Tremble, O heaven! be aghast, O earth! This presumption is worse than the former: the impiety the former then betrayed these people now betray, likewise adoring the creature; but what they have now come up with no single human being at that time presumed to claim or give credence to.[11] What are you saying? the vision was an example of considerateness? Yes, but God's considerateness: if Daniel, who enjoyed great confidence with God, could not bear to look upon an angel being considerate to him, but fell down and lay prostrate, with his body's sinews loosened,[12] what is remarkable if the seraphim are stricken with astonishment, unable to bear looking at that awesome glory? The distance between Daniel and the angel, after all, does not match that between God and those powers.

In case, however, by spending further time on these marvels we cast your soul into a stupor, come now, let us take the sermon back to the beginning of the story, and lead you forward with simpler accounts. "It was in the year that King Uzziah died." It is worth inquiring, firstly, why the inspired author indicates the time to us; he does not do it pointlessly or to no purpose. The mouths of the inspired authors are the mouth of God, after all; such a mouth would say nothing idly – so let us not be idle in our listening, either. [13] You see, if those who dig up metals do not pass over even tiny fragments, but on striking a vein of gold look around carefully for nuggets, much more should we do this in the case of the Scriptures. Admittedly, in the case of metals the search is very difficult for the prospectors: the metals are earth and the gold is nothing but earth, and their natural commonality deceives the eye of the prospectors; yet instead of desisting they give evidence of utter diligence, knowing as they do by sight what is really earth and what is really gold. In the case of Scripture, on the other hand, it is not like this: the gold does not lie mixed up with earth – it is pure gold. "The Lord's sayings are untainted," Scripture says, remember, "silver purified by fire, tested by earth" [14] – that is to say, the Scriptures are not metals that require hard labor; rather, they provide a treasure ready for those searching for the wealth coming from them. It is in fact sufficient merely to peep within, and go away filled with every benefit; it is sufficient only to open them, and at once discern the sparkle of the jewels.

Now, it is not idly that this is said by me, nor have I prolonged the treatment without purpose. It is because some people are mechanically-minded, and when they take the divine books in their hands and find dates and lists of names contained, [15] immediately they pass over them and say to their critics, It is all names, it contains nothing of value. What are you saying? God makes a statement, and you dare to claim, There is nothing useful in what is said? If you were simply to see a bare inscription, would you not stop still with interest and study the wealth contained in it? But why mention dates and names and inscriptions? Come to grasp the importance of the addition of a single syllable, and stop despising whole names. Our patriarch Abraham (he is ours, you know, rather than belonging to the Jews)[16] was first called Abram, which means traveler; later, with a change of name to Abraham, he became father of all the nations, and addition of a single syllable entrusted the good man with such a great responsibility.[17] In other words, just as the emperors bestow golden tablets on their viceroys as a symbol of authority, so too God on this occasion gave that good man the syllable as a sign of his status.

At another time, however, I shall treat of names. But there is need to mention the great value in knowing dates and the great harm in being ignorant of them. I shall demonstrate this firstly, for instance, from matters of daily life.[18] Wills and certificates to do with marriages, debts and other contracts, unless they bear the dates of the consulate on the front, are devoid of any inherent force: it is the date that is their authority, that removes any grounds for challenge, that keeps them out of the courts and makes enemies friends. Hence those who draw them up insert the consulate on the front page, like a lamp on a lamp-stand, (111) to shed light on all that follows. If you remove that, you remove the light, and plunge everything into darkness and great confusion. Hence all payment and receipt, whether involving friends or enemies, servants or trustees or managers, requires this security, and in every case we write down months and years and days. If, then, the practice has such force in affairs of daily life, in spiritual matters it is much more important and useful. It is, in fact, what proves prophecies to be prophecy: prophecy is nothing else than the prediction of future events.[19] How, then, will the person ignorant of the mention of events and outcomes be able to prove to the adversary the worth of the prophecy? From this fact come also our contests and victories against Greeks, when we demonstrate our things to be older than theirs; from this come also our demonstrations of the truth against Jews – the poor wretched Jews, who stumbled with the worst stumble on account of their ignorance of times. I mean, had they listened to the patriarch saying, "A ruler will not depart from Judah, nor a leader from his thighs, until he comes with whom it rests,"[20] and had they observed with precision the times of his coming, they would not have fallen out with the Christ and fallen in with the Anti-Christ. As Christ himself, therefore, also suggested to them in saying, "I came in my Father's name, and you did not receive me; if somebody else came in their own name, you would receive them."[21] Do you what see what an awful blunder came from the ignorance of times? So let us not be heedless of such great usefulness: just as boundaries and posts in the fields prevent allotments from being confused, so dates and times stop events from overlapping with one another, and by distinguishing one from another and putting each in its right order they preserve us from utter bewilderment.

It is therefore worth telling you who this Uzziah was, when he reigned, over whom he reigned, for how long his rule lasted, and how he ended his life – or, rather, it is worth keeping silence at this point; this involves launching our sermon onto the unbounded ocean of stories. Now, for those on the point of traveling on such an ocean the journey has to be commenced with the rowers not tired but at their peak. This is the reason that harbors and islands have sprung up at all points in the sea, for both pilot and seaman to take a rest, the one by setting aside the oar, the other by leaving the tiller; this is the reason that havens and inns are devised for all points along the road, for beasts and riders to rest from their efforts. This is also the reason that a moment of silence has been determined also in the words of instruction, in case we wear ourselves out with the plethora of language and bore you. Solomon also recognised these moments, saying, "A time for keeping silence, and a time for speaking."[22]

Let us, then, have a time for keeping silence so that the master may have a time for speaking: our words resemble wine recently drawn from the vat (112) whereas his are like wine aged and matured, providing great benefit and efficacy to the recipients. That Gospel maxim has been observed today: the better wine is served after the worse;[23] and just as it was no vine which produced that wine on that occasion but instead it was the result of the power of Christ, so too no human mind pours forth this man's speech, but the grace of the Spirit. Since the streams, then, are generous and spiritual, let us receive them with enthusiasm, let us observe them with diligence, so that we may be bedewed by them unceasingly and bear fruit in season to the God who regales us with them. To him belong all glory and honor, together with his only-begotten Son and the all-holy Spirit, now and forever, for ages of ages. Amen.

Homily Three
*On the passage in Chronicles which says,
"Uzziah's heart was lifted up."*[1]
On humility and the fact that the person of virtue ought not be overly-confident; and on the great evil that arrogance is.

Blessed be God for the emergence of martyrs in our time and for vouchsafing us the sight of people being put to death for Christ, dripping with holy blood to bedew the whole Church, dripping with blood that strikes fear into demons, arouses envy in angels and is salutary for us.[2] We have been vouchsafed to see people taking up the cudgels for religion and being crowned. We have been vouchsafed, however, not only to see but also to receive the very bodies of the athletes, and we now have the champions with us. But today we shall leave the sermon on the martyrs to the imitator of the martyrs, our own teacher,[3] while for the present we shall speak to you of the story of Uzziah, discharging a longstanding debt and concluding lengthy pangs of attentiveness; each of you suffers pangs, I well know, in anticipation of hearing that story, and we prolonged those pangs, not with the intention of aggravating the pangs but in our anxiety to deepen the longing so that our fare might strike you as most palatable. Wealthy hosts, after all, even if hosting guests already sated, would be capable of stimulating their appetite with the lavish hospitality, whereas nothing so makes the table of poor people look lavish as having those due to partake of it arrive starving.[4]

So who is Uzziah, whose descendant was he, over whom was he king, how long was he king, what good did he do and what sins commit, and how did he end his life? I shall now tell you all of this – or, rather, as much as is possible without confusing your memory with a huge amount. It is what happens also with the lamplight: if in that case you dispense the oil gradually onto the wick, you give the fire sufficient nourishment, whereas if you pour it on in one go, you also snuff out whatever fire there is.

This man Uzziah, then, was a descendant of David and king of the Jews, and he reigned for fifty-two years; well-thought of at first, (113) he later fell into sin: he formed ideas beyond his station, and encroached on the responsibility of priesthood.[5] Such is the full malice of arrogance: it causes one to be ignorant of oneself, and despite one's great efforts it completely empties the treasury of virtue. While the other vices generally get the better of us when we are negligent, this vice comes upon us in our good deeds: nothing is so accustomed to generate arrogance as a good conscience unless we are on our guard. Hence Christ also, aware that this passion attacks us after works of virtue, said to the disciples, "When you do this, say, We are unprofitable servants"[6] – that is, when this wild beast is on the point of attacking you, then by these words shut the door on it. He did not say, When you do this, you are unprofitable, but "say, We are unprofitable:" say it, do not be afraid I shall pass judgement on the basis of your opinion; if you declare yourself unprofitable, I shall crown you for being profitable. Likewise he also says elsewhere, "Tell your sins first so as to be justified."[7] In the case of secular courts, remember, after the accusation[8] of the sinner comes death, whereas in God's courts after the accusation of sins comes the crown. Hence Solomon also said, "Do not justify yourself before the Lord."[9]

Uzziah, however, was sensitive to none of this: he entered the Temple bent on offering incense, and did not desist when the priest opposed him. So what did God do? He afflicted him with leprosy on the forehead[10] to punish his shameless visage and to teach him that the court is divine and his war was not with human beings. This is what happened to Uzziah. Come now, let us take up the story from the beginning as well; the reason for my giving it in advance to you in a nutshell and telling all that happened was that when you hear Scripture reporting it you may follow it precisely. Now, pay attention. "Uzziah did what was right in the sight of the Lord,"[11] the text says. It testified in these words to his great virtue: he not only did what was right but also in the sight of the Lord, not as a display to human beings, not like those among the Jews who blow the trumpet before almsgiving, who disfigure their faces in fasting, who do their praying in the streets.[12] What could be more unfortunate than they, when they make such efforts, to be deprived of all reward? What are you doing, mortal that you are? are you bent on rendering an account of your doings to another, and calling on another as witness to what happens? do you have another judge, and put someone else in the position of observer? have you not noticed that the charioteers, when the whole city is seated above in the equestrian contests, cover the whole course of the stadium and vie with one another to overturn the chariots of their rivals at the point where they see the emperor seated, thinking one eye is more important than so many other faces? (114) Do you, by contrast, see the very king of the angels themselves judging your contests, yet shun him for the faces of your fellow slaves? Is this, to be sure, the reason why after so many contests you go away uncrowned, and go off to the judge bereft of trophies despite your many labors?

Uzziah, however, was not like that: he did what was right in the sight of the Lord. How was it, then, that after living his life so scrupulously, he stumbled and fell? I too, in fact, am amazed and at a loss about this – or, rather, it would not be something to be surprised at: he was a human being, after all, something prone to sin and inclined to vice. This is not the only problem: there is also the fact that we are bidden travel by a narrow and straitened way bordered on either side by precipices. Consequently, when ease of choice and difficulty of way come together, do not then be surprised at falls: just as at the spectacles those who practice going up and down a tightrope fall head over heels into the pit if they look away for an instant, and lose their life, so too those traveling by this way come to grief if they relax for an instant. This way, in fact, is narrower and straighter than that rope, and steeper and much higher: it reaches to heaven itself, and our steps will then be more secure when we arrive up there at the very peak. Those standing on heights, of course, have a deep fear, and there is only one safe way left to them, not to look down or glance at the ground, an awful dizziness coming from that.

This is the reason, to be sure, that the inspired author ceaselessly cries out to us in the words, "Do not lose everything at the end," stirring up our slothful spirit, checking it when it is on the verge of falling, and invigorating it.[13] In the beginning, you see, we do not need much encouragement. Why on earth? Because every person, even if the most sluggish of all, when on the point of commencing a project gives evidence of great zeal at the outset, and with enthusiasm waxing and faculties still fresh they easily apply themselves to their purpose. But when we have covered much of the journey, and the force of our enthusiasm wanes, our faculties tire and we are on the point of collapsing, then it is that the inspired author brings timely support, offering this maxim like a kind of staff, saying, "Do not lose everything at the end." The devil, you see, pants more fiercely at that time: just as the pirates plying the sea do not make an attack when the ships are leaving port (what good would it do them if the vessel went down empty?) but adopt every means when they come back with a full cargo, so too that wicked demon on seeing us with a collection of many virtues – fasting, prayer, almsgiving, self-control and all the rest – then makes his move when he sees our vessel loaded with the valuable jewels of piety, plundering the treasure at all points, with the result that the vessel sinks at the very mouth of the harbor, and (115) then casts us up in port empty-handed. Hence the inspired author's urging everyone in the words, "Do not lose everything at the end." After such a fall recovery in due course is not easy, in fact: "The person falling to the depths of vice becomes contemptuous,"[14] remember. While we all make allowances for the person falling at the beginning on account of inexperience, one would not readily concede pardon or excuse to the one stumbling after much practice: the fall at that stage seems to be the result of indifference. That is not the worst of it: there is the fact that many people are also scandalised by the falls of such people, and so the sin is unpardonable on this score as well.

Aware of all this, then, let us give heed to the inspired author, and not lose everything at the end, this being the reason that Ezekiel also cries out in the words, "If someone is righteous and then lapses into sin, instead of their righteous behavior being remembered they will die in their sin;"[15] he too was afraid of the end, note. Not only on this score: from the opposite case as well he brings out the real seriousness of the situation: "If someone is a sinner and then is converted and becomes righteous, their righteous behavior will not be remembered; thanks to their righteousness they will live."[16] Note in this case, too, the great attention he pays to the end: lest the righteous trust in their righteousness, slip into indifference and be lost, he frightens them with a reference to the end; lest sinners despair at the thought of their falls and remain forever in their fallen state, he revives them with a reference to the end, saying, Your sins are many, but do not despair: recovery is possible if you prove the end is the opposite of the beginning. He says in turn to the righteous, Your virtuous deeds are many, but do not grow over-confident: you can fall as well if you do not take equal care for the end. Do you see how he canceled one person's indifference and the other's despair?

Uzziah was sensitive to nothing of this; hence he also grew over-confident and sustained a grave and incurable fall. Not every fall, you see, causes us the same wound: some sins subject us to reproof, whereas others earn us the harshest of penalties. Those who did not wait for their brethren in the common meals, for instance, Paul upbraided in these terms, "In giving this instruction I do not commend you."[17] Do you see how the sin stopped short at reproof and received censure as the penalty? But he does not react this way when speaking about fornication. How, then? "If anyone destroys the temple of God, God will destroy that person."[18] In this case, note, instead of censure or reproof there is the harshest punishment. Solomon was also aware of the differences in sins, distinguishing theft from adultery, for instance, when speaking in these terms, "It is not surprising if someone is caught stealing: they steal to fill their hungry spirit; but the adulterer brings ruin on his own spirit from lack of brains."[19] Each is a sin, he is saying, but one less and one greater: one person has the excuse of need, the other is devoid of any pretext.

But, you may object, the latter feels (116) the pressure of natural desire. The wife allotted to him, on the contrary, does not allow this latitude: she opposes it by depriving him of any excuse. This, in fact, is the reason for marriage and lawful enjoyment of it, that a husband may not be able to make any such claim; the reason a wife was given to him was for him to repress nature's frenzy so as to calm the billows of desire.[20] Just as a steersman, then, responsible for shipwreck in port would not be conceded any excuse, so too the person who despite the security of being married intrudes into another man's marriage or passes a roving eye over any woman at all would not be allowed an excuse by human beings or by God, even if time without number he cited natural pleasure as a pretext. Rather, what pleasure could there be where there is fear and anguish, danger and expectation of such awful troubles, courts and liabilities, a judge's wrath, sword and executioner, dungeon and gibbet? Such a man dreads and trembles at everything – shadows, walls, the very stones – as though giving voice; he imagines and suspects everyone – servants, neighbors, friends, enemies, people who know something, people who know nothing.

But if you please, suppose all this is done with and no one knows what happened except the man alone together with the woman who has been abused: how will he bear the accusation of conscience, carrying around with him everywhere its harsh condemnation? I mean, as you could not avoid yourself, so he cannot avoid the verdict of that awesome tribunal, either. That court is not swayed by bribes, it does not yield to flattery: it is God's court, and has been placed within our souls by God. In very truth "the adulterer brings ruin on his own spirit from lack of brains." Admittedly, the thief, far from being rid of punishment, pays a penalty, but it is less. Comparisons, you see, do not force the things compared to take the position of opposites: they allow them to remain as they are, but introduce the notion of defect and excess. Perhaps you have not understood what has been said; so I must make it clearer. Marriage is good, but virginity is better: it is not that marriage is bad because virginity is better – just that it is less than the other, though good in itself. So too in this case: theft is bad, but while it is less so than the other, it is bad also in itself.

Do you see the differences in sins? Let us see, then, what kind of sin this man committed. "His heart was lifted up," the text says. A severe wound: arrogance it is – arrogance, the source of all vices. For you to learn concisely the evil of this ailment, listen to this. While the other sins have to do with our nature, pride dragged down an incorporeal power and dislodged it from on high: this it was that made the devil to be the devil at a time when he was not the devil. If, on the one hand, we cite Isaiah as witness in his words about him, "I shall rise up to heaven, and I shall be like the most high," those not happy to accept allegories will reject our testimony;[21] if, on the other hand, we call Paul to prosecute him, no one will have any further objections. So what does Paul say in writing to Timothy? That it was not proper to promote someone who had recently embraced the message to the high position of episcopacy; (117) he put it this way, "Not a neophyte in case he be puffed up and fall victim to condemnation and the devil's snare,"[22] meaning, in case he commit the same sin as he and suffer the same fate as he.

It is clear not only from this case but also from what that wicked demon advised the first of all human beings. You see, as it is customary with good people to recommend to their neighbors the things by which they themselves became good, so also it is customary with evil people to introduce to their neighbors the kinds of things by which they themselves turned bad. This, in fact, is one form of evil, to take the ruin of others as consolation for one's own punishment. So what did the devil advise Adam? To form an inflated idea of his own nature and aspire to equality with God:[23] if this forced me out of heaven, he said to himself, much more will this same thing force this creature out of paradise. Hence Solomon also said, "God resists the proud."[24] He did not say, God dismisses the proud, abandons them, deprives them of his assistance; instead, he says, Resists – not that he requires battle array and assault against the proud: what could be weaker than the proud? I mean, just as the one who has lost sight is vulnerable to abuse by everyone, so the proud, those who do not acknowledge the Lord ("Not acknowledging the Lord is the beginning of pride,"[25] Scripture says, remember) are easy prey also to human beings, having lost that light. But even if they should be strong, God would not need a battle array against them: his willing sufficed to produce everything, and so much more would it be sufficient also for their removal. Why then, you ask, does he resist? To indicate the depth of his abhorrence for the proud.

While the fact that the effect of pride is disastrous emerges from this and from other evidence, therefore, yet if you do not mind, let us learn the cause of the trouble also from other sources. I mean, it is customary with Scripture, when it is about to accuse someone, not only to mention their sin but to teach us also the cause of the sin; it does this to make the healthy more careful not to fall into the same sins. Likewise, too, physicians attending patients trace the source even before the onset of the ailments so as to check the problem from the outset; the one who only cuts the growth while the root is untouched simply wastes his time. So how did Scripture mention the sin and the cause of the sin? It accuses the people before the flood of improper intercourse: listen to the way it cites the cause. "When the sons of God saw that the daughters of human beings were beautiful, they took them as wives for themselves."[26] So what: was beauty the cause of the sin? Perish the thought: it is a work of God's wisdom, and a work of God would never be a cause of wickedness. Well, looking at it? Not that, either: this, too, is a work of nature. Well, what?

Looking at it wrongly: this comes from a corrupt attitude. Hence a sage also advises in these words, "Do not become familiar with a beauty belonging to another."[27] He did not say, Do not look: this can even happen without willing; (118) instead, "Do not become familiar," eliminating the deliberate attention, the roving eye, the evil glance to pass the time that comes from a corrupt and lustful spirit. And what harm could come from this, you ask? "From this," the sage continues, "love is enkindled like fire:" just as fire, when it takes hold of hay or chaff, wastes no time, and instead as soon as it grips the material it bursts into a bright flame, so too the fire of lust within us, when by the faculty of sight it seizes upon a pleasing and sparkling beauty, immediately set the soul alight. Have no eye, then, for passing pleasure that comes from sight; consider rather the unending pain that comes from lust: while it often takes its leave after inflicting the wound, the wound does not take its leave, but often abides and brings ruin. And as a deer with a shaft in its vitals eludes the hands of the hunters all to no avail, so too a soul pierced with a shaft from undisciplined and idle gazing, even if it dislodges the shaft and goes off, is mortally affected and perishes, seeing the enemy everywhere and keeping it in its wake.

What I was saying, however (we should not allow ourselves to indulge in long digressions), that Scripture is accustomed to mention the sins and their causes, listen for instance here as well to what it says about Uzziah. It not only taught us, note, that his heart was lifted up, but added also whence it was lifted up. Whence was it lifted up, then? "When he became strong," it says, "his heart was lifted up." He could not cope with the importance of his position: just as indigestion comes from over-eating, and fever is produced by indigestion, and then death often results from that, so too in this case from the great pressure of affairs arrogance resulted: what indigestion is in bodies, arrogance is in souls. Then from arrogance a longing for things not proper to him.

Far from there being no purpose in our taking this to great length, our intention is that you may never regard as enviable or blessed those in a high position, in the knowledge of the great instability involved; that you may never consider wretched those in need and hardship, in the knowledge of the greater security coming from it. Hence the inspired author also cries out, "It is good for me, O Lord, that you have humbled me."[28] Note, at any rate, how great the evil that came from a lofty position: "His heart was lifted up to the point of destruction." What is the meaning of "to the point of destruction"? While some evil thoughts do not invade the soul at all if we obstruct them with great care, others develop within when we are negligent, and grow; but if we anticipate them, they are quickly suffocated and overcome. Still others develop and grow up and issue in evil actions, and they quickly destroy our health of soul when we fall into complete negligence. So this is what is meant by "his heart was lifted up;" and instead of remaining within and being snuffed out, the arrogance (119) had an evil outcome, destroying his virtue completely. It is a blessed thing, therefore, not to give admittance of any kind to the evil thought – hence the inspired author's also saying, "Lord, my heart is not lifted up."[29] He did not say, My heart was lifted up but I repressed it; instead, Not even at the outset was it lifted up – that is, I always kept my soul from the inroads of vice. While this, then, is a blessed thing, next to it comes promptly repelling those that enter, and not allowing them more time there lest they have a bad effect on us. If, however, we should be negligent even to this point, there is the possibility of consolation even for this negligence, thanks to God's lovingkindness, and by that great and ineffable goodness many remedies have been prepared for those wounds.

But come now, let us bring this discourse to a close lest

what I feared in the beginning may occur, and the multitude of words affect your memory. Hence there is need also to sum up briefly what was said, which is what mothers do: when they put fruits and sweets and similar things into a child's lap, they use a belt to make its tunic safe by tightening it all around so that none of the things given to it may fall out through the child's negligence. Let us do this, too, let us compress the sermon that went to great length, and leave it in the custody of your memory. You heard how nothing should be done for display, what a great evil negligence is, how easily it tripped up even the one living an exact life. You recognised how much zeal this requires of us, particularly towards the end of life, and how neither the one who repented of falls should despair nor the one grown indifferent in the practice of virtue should be overly confident. We discoursed to you on the differences in sins, on not hankering after bodily splendor, and we showed how great an evil this involved. You remember our words on arrogance, and on bad thoughts. [30]

Holding fast to this, let us head homewards – or, rather, holding fast to this let us receive also the more accomplished exhortation of the excellent teacher: while ours – such as it is – shows traces of youth, his – whatever it proves to be – is decked with hoary wisdom; while ours is like a wildly rushing torrent, his is like a fountain releasing rivers in great tranquillity, resembling the flow of oil rather than water. Let us therefore receive the streams so that they may become in us a source of water gushing up to life eternal. [31] May it be the good fortune of us all to attain this, thanks to the grace and lovingkindness of our Lord Jesus Christ, to whom with the Father and the holy and good Spirit be honor, glory and might, now and forever, for ages of ages. Amen.

Homily Four

*On the verse of the prophet Isaiah that says,
"In the year that King Uzziah died I saw
the Lord seated on a lofty and exalted throne."
Also, a eulogy of the city of Antioch, and an inspired
proof against those who forbid marriage.*

A distinguished spectacle was provided for us today and (120) a splendid assembly. Whatever, then, was responsible for it? Today's harvest is the crop from yesterday's seed; yesterday we planted, today we gather. It is not lifeless ground we are tending for a late yield, you see, but rational souls, it is not tardy nature but lively grace. Our people are orderly, the congregation attentive.[1] Yesterday they were called, and today they are crowned; the fruit of yesterday's exhortation is today's responsiveness. Hence we for our part sow the seed with enthusiasm because we see the pasture clean, nowhere suffocating thorns, nor trampled path, nor sterile rock: only a deep and fertile furrow, receiving the seeds and yielding us the ear of grain.[2]

This is my constant claim, and I shall never cease saying it, that the glory of this city is not that it has a senate,[3] not that we have consuls in our ranks, nor many statues, nor an abundance of merchandise, nor a suitable location; rather, its glory is that it has a responsive public, temples which God occupies, and that the Church delights rather in a word that streams forth daily and a longing never sated. In short, the city is admired not for its buildings but for its inhabitants. Do not tell me that the city of the Romans is great in size: show me a people equally attentive to be found there. Sodom had its towers, too, while a hut held Abraham; but when the angels came, they bypassed Sodom and lodged in the hut,[4] not interested in splendor of dwellings but going about in search of virtue and beauty of soul. We find the same thing elsewhere: the desert played host to John,[5] the city to Herod; hence the desert was more hospitable than the city. Why on earth? Because the charism of inspiration is not to be found in created things.

Now, I say this in case we ever eulogise a city morally dissolute. Why quote me buildings and columns? These tumble in the present life. Go into church and see the city's true nobility. Go in, take note of the needy staying there from midnight till daylight, see the sacred vigils linking day to night, respecting the tyranny of sleep neither by day nor by night, nor the pressure of need. A great city, the world's metropolis: how many bishops, how many teachers have come there and gone off, having learnt lessons from the people and prepared to transplant the law that has taken root there. If you quote me high office and abundance of possessions, you are basing your praise on the foliage, not on the fruit. I say this, however, not to flatter your good selves but to proclaim your virtue. I am blessed in you; you are blessed in yourselves. "Blessed is the one who speaks to attentive ears:"[6] thus have I been blessed. "Blessed are those who hunger and thirst for righteousness:"[7] see how you are blessed in yourselves.

Blessed is the man who loves spiritual discourse; this is what differentiates us from brute beasts – not, in fact, bodily resemblance, (121) eating and drinking, being territorial and living, all these being shared by us with brute beasts. What is it, rather, by which the human being is distinguished from the beasts? Language: on this score the human being is also a rational being.[8] In other words, just as bodies are fed, so the soul is also fed – but the body on bread and the soul on language. So if you saw human beings eating stone, surely you would not class them as human? Likewise, if you saw them nourished not on language but on silence, you would say, They have lost their humanity as well, the nourishment revealing the human being's nobility.

Since, then, our theatre is full or, to put it differently, the heaving sea is awash with tranquillity or, again, the storm-tossed ocean is steady – come now, let us launch the boat, unfurling our tongue in place of the sail, calling on the grace of the Spirit in place of the breeze, employing as pilot the Cross instead of rudder and oar. While the sea has water that is brackish, here there is living water. There you find brute beasts, here rational souls; there the travelers go from sea to land, here the travelers leave the earth and put in at heaven; there boats, here spiritual discourses; there planks in the boat, here tightly-welded discourses; there a sail, here a tongue; there a breath of air, here a visit from the Spirit; there a human pilot, here the pilot is Christ. Hence, though storm-tossed, the boat does not sink: while the boat could spend the passage in tranquillity, the pilot would not allow it, his purpose being for you to see the endurance of the travelers and gain a precise understanding of the pilot's skill. [9]

Let Greeks give heed, let Jews give heed to our works of virtue and the Church's pre-eminence. How many enemies has the Church faced without ever being overcome? how many tyrants? how many generals? how many emperors – Augustus, Tiberius, Gaius, Claudius, Nero, people lauded to the skies, people of power – waged such awful war on a recent bloom without uprooting it? [10] Instead, the warmongers are not mentioned and are consigned to oblivion, whereas their victim rises above the heavens. Are you not aware of this, I ask you, that the Church is placed on earth but its life is lived in heaven? How does this emerge? The facts give clear proof: eleven disciples were under attack, and the whole world did the attacking; but those attacked had the victory, and the attackers were done away with. The sheep prevailed over the wolves: do you see the shepherd sending the sheep amidst the wolves so that they would not achieve salvation even by flight? What sort of shepherd does this? Christ did it, however, to show you that good deeds are done not in the normal course of events but in defiance of nature and normal events. The Church's roots, in fact, are stronger than heaven. But perhaps the Greek charges me with arrogance: let him await factual proof and learn (122) the force of the truth, how the sun would more easily be snuffed out than the Church disappear. Who proclaims this, you ask? Its founder: "Heaven and earth will pass away, but my words will not pass away."[11] Instead of simply making this promise, he actually brought it to fulfilment; after all, why did he give it a firmer foundation than heaven? The Church, you see, is more important than heaven. For what reason does heaven exist? For the Church, not the Church for heaven. Heaven is for the human being, not the human being for heaven. This is clear from what he actually did: Christ did not take up a heavenly body.

In case we prolong the sermon, however, let us again today go off as debtors (you know how much we promised yesterday) ready to settle the account; it was due to those absent that we delayed doing so.[12] Since the absent have done their duty, then, and by their presence have regaled us with a table of costly fare – come now, let us provide the seasoning, a seasoning that has not gone stale; after all, if it were yesterday's, it would not be seasoning. What on earth is it? It is not meat, something that could perish, but ideas that are constantly flowering. Meats perish, of course, being material, whereas thoughts continue in existence and become more fragrant. So what was it that we said yesterday? For our part, in fact, we did enjoy yesterday's banquet, and the absent are none the worse for it. "In the year that King Uzziah died I saw the Lord seated on a lofty and exalted throne." Who says this? Isaiah, ambassador of the seraphim, who had experience of marriage without extinguishing grace. You have paid attention to the prophet; well, listen to the prophet today as well, "Go out, you and your son Jashub."[13] This should not be passed over, either. "Go out, you and your son:" did the prophet have a son? So if he had a son, he also had a wife, the message for you being that marriage is not base: it is fornication that is evil.

When we speak to the general run of people, however, and say, Why do you not live properly? why not give evidence of an exact life? How can I, they reply, unless I leave my wife, unless I leave my children, unless I leave my business? Why so? Surely marriage is no hindrance? Your wife is given to you as a help, not a schemer; did not the prophet have a wife? Marriage was no obstacle to the Spirit; he had experience of marriage and was a prophet as well. Did not Moses have a wife? He split rocks, transformed the sky, spoke with God and checked divine anger. Did not Abraham have a wife? He became the father of nations and of the Church. Isaac in fact was his son: did he not prove the occasion for virtuous actions? Did he not make an offering of his son, the fruit of his marriage? was he not both father and lover of God? can we not see him becoming a priest from his own feelings? priest and father? nature overcome and devotion triumphant? feelings trampled on and pious deeds prevailing? the father laid low and the lover of God crowned? do you not see in one person lover of his child and lover of God? surely marriage offered no obstacle?[14]

And what of the mother of the (123) Maccabees: was she not a wife? did she not give seven sons as the group of holy ones? did she not see them martyred? did she not remain immovable like a mountain? did she not remain firm as she was martyred in the case of each of them, mother of martyrs and seven times martyred? While they were tortured, it was she in fact who felt the blows. It was not, of course, without feelings that she thus accepted what happened: she was a mother, and the force of nature made itself felt – but she was not overcome. She was, in fact, ocean and billows; and as the ocean, when enraged, becomes calm, so too nature, when stirred, is reined in by the fear of God. How did she anoint them? how did she raise them? how did she present seven temples to God, golden statues – or, rather, more precious than gold? For proof, you see, that gold is not like the soul of martyrs, pay attention. The tyrant stood there, and overcome by one single woman he yielded; he laid siege with weapons, she prevailed with zeal; he lit the furnace, she the virtue of the Spirit; he deployed an army, she sought refuge with angels. She saw the tyrant here-below, and imagined the one reigning on high; she saw the tortures here-below, and calculated the prizes on high; she saw the present punishment, and imagined the future immortality. Hence Paul also said, "We consider not what can be seen but what cannot be seen."[15]

Surely marriage proved no hindrance? What of Peter, the foundation of the Church, the wild lover of Christ, unskilled in the word and overwhelming orator, unlettered yet stopping the mouths of philosophers, undoing the pagan religion like a spider web, traversing the whole world, fishing the sea and landing the world – did he too not have a wife? Yes, he did; for proof that he had one, listen to the evangelist. Now, what does he say? "Jesus went in to see Peter's mother-in-law, who had a fever:"[16] where there is a mother in law, there is also a wife, and where a wife, also marriage. And what of Philip? did he not have four daughters?[17] Where there are four daughters, there is also a wife and marriage. So what of Christ? Born of a virgin, admittedly, but he went to a wedding and gave a present: "They have no wine,"[18] Scripture says, remember, and he turned the water into wine, dignifying the wedding with his virginity, honoring the function with his gift, to prevent you looking down on marriage while hating fornication.

At my own risk I guarantee your salvation, wife or no wife. Take heed to your own situation: if your wife is useful, she is your helpmate. So what if she is not useful? Make her useful. Were there not good wives and bad, a fact that prevents your having an excuse? What sort was Job's? Sarah, on the other hand, was good. I shall give you the case of a vile and wicked wife. Did Job's wife not harm her husband? She was vile and wicked, and urged him to blaspheme. (124) So what happened: did she shake the tower? dislodge the immovable? overcome the rock? smite the soldier? hole the vessel? uproot the tree? None of these: she struck, and the tower became more steady; she stirred up the billows, but instead of the vessel sinking, it sailed on with a fair wind; its fruit was plucked, but the tree did not topple; the leaves fell, but the root remained unmoved. I tell you this in case anyone should offer the excuse of a wife's wickedness. Is she vile? Set her right. But, you say, she drove me out of paradise. Still, she also brought you into heaven. While the nature is the same, the will is different. But Job's wife was vile, you claim? Yet Susanna was good. But the Egyptian woman was lascivious, you claim? Yet Sarah was demure. Do you see the one? take note also of the the other, since among men as well some are vile while others are devoted: Joseph was good, but the elders lascivious.[19] You see vice and virtue everywhere, not determined by nature but differentiated by free will. Excuse yourself to me with no excuses.

Let us show some concern, however, for the debt and its repayment. "In the year that King Uzziah died." I am about to explain why the inspired author indicates the time. Yesterday, remember, we wondered why on earth it is that, when all the inspired authors including this one customarily mention the time of the king's life, there is here a departure from the custom: he speaks not of the lifetime of Uzziah but of the death of Uzziah.[20] I intend to solve this today. Even if the temperature is high, you see, the dew from the sermon is greater: even if the body that is pampered finds the going heavy, the soul that is vigorous is exhilarated. Do not speak to me of heat and sweat: if your body is sweating, sponge your mind. The three young men were in the furnace without suffering anything, and instead the furnace turned to dew.[21] When you think of sweat, think also of payment and reward: a diver risks plunging himself to the depths of the sea for no other purpose than pearls, the cause of war. I have no quarrel with the material thing, however – just the undisciplined attitude. And you for your part, for the sake of receiving an unfailing treasure and planting a vine in your soul, would you not put up with heat or sweat? have you not noticed the people sitting in the theatre, how they sweat and bear the brunt of the sun's rays for the sake of falling captive to death, of being in thrall to a prostitute? do they exert themselves for their undoing, while you are lax about your salvation? You are an athlete and a soldier; so instead of exerting yourself to your peril, see the struggle through to the end in good spirits.[22]

Who, then, is this Uzziah, and why does this death of his rate a mention? This Uzziah was a king, a righteous man with many good deeds to his credit; but at some later stage he fell into arrogance – into arrogance, the mother of vices, into presumption, the confused state of mind of the ill, into pride, the devil's downfall. Nothing, in fact, is worse than arrogance – hence our spending all the sermon (125) yesterday on this subject to rid us of arrogance and teach us humility.[23] Should I tell you what a great good humility is and what an awful evil arrogance? A sinner surpassed a righteous person, the tax collector the pharisee, words did better than deeds. How did words succeed? The tax collector says, "O God, be merciful to me, a sinner;" the pharisee says, "I am not like the rest of people, rapacious, greedy" – instead, what? "I fast twice a week, I give away a tenth of my possessions."[24] The pharisee highlighted deeds of righteousness, the tax collector spoke words of humility, and words got the better of deeds, such a great treasure went up in thin air and such great poverty was transformed into wealth. Two ships arrived carrying cargo, both entered the harbor; but the tax collector docked successfully in port while the pharisee suffered shipwreck, the lesson for you being the awful evil arrogance is. Are you righteous? Do not humble your brethren. Have you good deeds to your credit? Do not reproach your neighbor and undermine the compliments due you. However great you are, humble yourself the more.

Give precise attention to the story, dearly beloved. The righteous person has reason to fear arrogance more than the sinner; I said so yesterday, and I say it today on account of those absent yesterday.[25] Hence the sinner has conscience to accuse him and is forced to humble himself, whereas the righteous person is carried away with virtuous actions. Just as in the case of ships, then, those that have an empty hold are not afraid of a band of pirates, as they do not come to sink the ship carrying nothing, whereas those with a full hold are afraid of pirates, as the pirate goes where there is gold, silver, precious stones, so too the devil is a ready threat not to the sinner but to the righteous, where there is great wealth. Since arrogance is often due to the devil's scheming, there is need to be on the alert. However great you are, humble yourself the more. When you climb the heights, you have need to take precautions against falling. Hence our Lord also says, "When you have done everything, say, We are unprofitable servants."[26] Why are you self-important, mortal as you are, related to the earth, of the same substance as ashes in nature, attitude and choice of things? Today wealthy, tomorrow poor; today healthy, tomorrow ill; today happy, tomorrow sad; today esteemed, tomorrow dishonored; today youthful, tomorrow old. Surely there is nothing human that stands firm; instead, it resembles the flow of the river's streams: as soon as it appears, it forsakes us more quickly than a shadow. So why are you self-important, mortal that you are, smoke, futility? "Human beings are like futility," remember, "their days are like grass; the grass fades and its bloom falls."[27]

I say this, not to disparage your being, but to check your

arrogance: a human being is a wonderful thing, and a merciful man estimable. This man Uzziah, however, king as he was and wearing a diadem, was righteous, and so he somehow became self-important, and when his self-importance grew beyond his position, he entered the Temple. What does Scripture say? (126) He entered the Holy of Holies and said, I intend to offer incense. Already a king, he lays hold of the office of priesthood: I intend to offer incense, he says, since I am righteous. Keep to your proper limits, nonetheless: the limits of kingship are of one kind, the limits of priesthood another – but the latter surpass the former. A king's status, you see, does not depend on visible things, nor ought a king be designated on the basis of jewels attached to his person or gold he wears. He is in fact appointed to administer things on earth; the institution of priesthood, on the other hand, is established on high: "whatever you bind on earth will be bound also in heaven."[28] The king is entrusted with things here-below, I with heavenly things (when I say "I," I mean the priest).

So if you see an unworthy priest, do not criticise the priesthood: one should not criticise the office – just the one exercising a good office badly, since Judas also proved a traitor, yet this was a fault not of apostleship but of his free will, not a charge against priesthood but against the evil of free will. In your case, therefore, do not criticise the priesthood but the priest exercising a good office badly. Similarly, when someone is talking to you and says, Do you see this Christian? reply, I am talking to you not about persons, however, but about things. Likewise, how many physicians prove quacks, and give poisons instead of medicines? It is not the profession I am criticising, however, but the one practising the profession badly. How many sailors have sunk ships? It is not navigation, however, but their evil disposition. And if a Christian is a wretch, do not criticise the doctrine or the priesthood but the one adopting a good thing badly. The king is entrusted with bodies, the priest with souls; the king remits the balance of debts, the priest the balance of sins; the former obliges, the latter exhorts; the former by pressure, the latter by free will; the former has material weapons, the latter spiritual weapons; the former wages war on savages, the latter on demons. The latter office is higher; hence the king submits his head to the priest's hands, and at all points in the Old dispensation priests anointed kings.

That king, by contrast, transgressed the boundaries proper to him, infringed the measure of kingship, tried to extend it and entered the sanctuary on his own authority in his wish to offer incense. So what did the priest do? "It is not permitted to you, Uzziah, to offer incense."[29] Note the forthrightness, the independent mien, the language aspiring to heaven, the unassailable freedom, angelic mind in a human body, striding the earth but living a life in heaven. He saw the king, but had no eyes for the purple; he saw the king, but had no eyes for the diadem; quote me not kingship where there is transgression. "It is not permitted to you, O King, to offer incense in the Holy of Holies:" you violate boundaries, you look for what has not been given you – hence you will lose what you have. To offer incense is permitted not to you but to the priests; it is not your role but mine. Surely I did not wrest the purple from you? Do not wrest the priesthood from me.

"To offer incense is not permitted to you but to the priests, the sons of Aaron." This happened after a long time, after the death of Aaron. Why did he not only mention the priests but recall also the father? As it happened, something similar had occurred at that time: Dathan, Abiram and Korah rebelled against Aaron; the earth opened up and swallowed them; (127) fire came from on high and consumed them.[30] His wish, then, was to remind them of that story, that at one time they had abused the priesthood without being overcome; the multitude rose up, however, and God took vengeance on them, saying, "To offer incense is not permitted to you but to the priests, the sons of Aaron."[31] He did not say, Consider what those who did this at that time suffered; he did not say, Consider that the rebels were burnt alive. Instead, he mentioned Aaron's vindication and reminded them of his place in the story, as if to say, Do not presume to do what Dathan did lest you suffer the things that happened in Aaron's time.

King Uzziah, however, did not withdraw: puffed up with arrogance he entered the sanctuary and threw open the Holy of Holies in his wish to offer incense. So what did God do? Since, therefore, the priest had been treated badly, and priesthood's status trampled underfoot, the priest could do nothing more; after all, it is the role of a priest only to deliver a reproof and give evidence of forthrightness, not to take up arms, raise a shield, brandish a spear, draw a bow, discharge an arrow – only to deliver a reproof and give evidence of forthrightness. So since the priest had delivered a reproof, but the king did not yield and instead took up arms, shields and spears, and invoked the resources at his disposal, the priest said, I have done my best, I can do no more; come to the aid of priesthood insulted; laws are being violated, institutions overturned. So what did the loving God do? He punished the presumptuous one: "Immediately leprosy broke out on his forehead."[32] Where there was shameless temerity, there also retribution.

Do you see the lovingkindness in God's retribution? He did not release a thunderbolt, he did not cause an earthquake, he did not set the sky in disarray; instead, the leprosy broke out, and in no other place than his forehead, in order that he might bear the trophy of punishment so that it would be like an inscription on a column. It was not for his sake, you see, that it happened, but for people afterwards: he was capable of inflicting a punishment that was deserved, but did not inflict it; instead, it stood like an edict on some lofty place proclaiming, Do not do likewise in case you suffer a like punishment. He went forth as a living edict, his forehead emitting a sound more strident than any trumpet, an inscription written on his forehead, an indelible inscription: it was not written in ink for someone to delete it; instead, the leprosy came from nature and rendered him also unclean so as to make the others clean. Just as the condemned, when they get the noose, are led out with the rope in their mouth, so too this man in issuing forth had instead of a noose leprosy on his forehead since he had abused the priesthood. I say this to disparage not kingship but those carried away with arrogance and rage, so that you may learn that priesthood is greater than kingship. (128)

It is always God's practice when the soul sins, you see, to punish the body. He acted likewise in the case of Cain. His soul sinned by committing murder, and his body was disabled – and rightly so. Why? "You will be groaning and trembling on the earth,"[33] the text says. Cain went round communicating with everyone, giving voice in silence, voicelessly instructing. His tongue was silent but his body language was strident, he communicated to everyone the reason for his groaning, the reason for his trembling. Whereas Moses said as much in writing,[34] this man by his actions went about saying to everyone, "Do not kill." Do you see the silent mouth and strident actions? do you see a living edict carried around? do you see a walking monument? do you see the absence of retribution?[35] do you see punishment made the basis for instruction? do you see a soul in sin and flesh undergoing punishment? And rightly so. This was the case also with Zechariah: the soul sinned and the tongue was held fast;[36] the tongue having proved to be a useless instrument, the man who produced the voice (Zechariah) was punished – as the one who sinned (Uzziah) developed leprosy on the forehead to teach him a lesson. The king departed, having been made an example for everyone, the sanctuary was cleansed, he was driven out with no one expelling him; aspiring to the priesthood that was beyond him, he lost what he had. He left the sanctuary. While in olden times it was the law that every leper be expelled from the city,[37] it is no longer so. Why? When God was giving laws to children, as it were, leprosy was then bodily, whereas today it is leprosy of the soul that is in question. So the king left with leprosy, and out of respect for his diadem and the kingship they did not expel him from the city; instead he kept the throne in defiance of the law. So what did God do? In his rage against the Jews he put a stop to the charism of inspiration.

Now, all this is the result of the verse from the prophet, so that I may discharge my debt. Let us, however, return to the subject in hand.[38] The king left the sanctuary on being struck with leprosy. So although as unclean he should have been expelled from the city as well in keeping with custom, the populace permitted him to reside within and made no gesture, slight or great, as required by way of forthrightness. Since they allowed him that liberty, therefore, God turned away from them and put a stop to the charism of inspiration – and rightly so: in return for their breaking his law and being reluctant to expel the unclean one, he brought the charism of inspiration to a halt. "The word was precious at that time, and there was no inspired utterance,"[39] that is, God was not speaking through the inspired authors: the Spirit through whom they made utterance was not inspiring them since they kept the unclean one, (129) the Spirit's grace not being active in the case of unclean people. Hence he kept his distance, he did not reveal himself to the inspired authors: he was silent and remained hidden. For this saying to be clear, I shall make it obvious with an example. Just as a person well-disposed to someone, who deals him a mindless injury in some matter, says to him, I shall see you no more, I shall not speak to you, so too did God behave on this occasion: since they had angered him by not expelling Uzziah, he said, I shall no longer speak to your inspired authors, I shall no longer send the grace of the Spirit. Note a punishment conspicuous for its mildness: he did not send thunderbolts, he did not shake the city to its foundation; instead, what? You are not prepared to avenge me? I shall have no dealings with you. Surely I was capable of expelling him, after all? I chose to leave to you, however, what remained to be done. You refuse? I shall have no dealings with you, either, nor move the soul of the inspired authors. The grace of the Spirit was not active, it was silent, enmity between God and man.

When afterwards that man died, therefore, the reason for the curse also lapsed. So the prophet had passed a long time without prophesying; but at that man's death the wrath was dissipated and the charism of inspiration returned. The prophet now of necessity indicates the time in the words, "In the year King Uzziah died, I saw the Lord seated on a lofty and exalted throne:" when he died, then I saw the Lord. I did not see God before, note, because he was angry with us; the death of the unclean one happened, and dissolved the anger. Hence, though in all other places he mentions kings' lives, here it is Uzziah's end to which he refers:[40] "In the year King Uzziah died, I saw the Lord seated on a lofty and exalted throne." As well, however, it is possible to see here God's lovingkindness: the unclean one died, and God was reconciled with human beings. What is the reason that, though there were no virtuous actions, it still happened at his death? Because he is loving, and does not keep a precise account of such things; the loving and good God was interested in one thing alone, that the unclean one should leave.

Aware of this, therefore, let us banish arrogance, embrace humility and offer the customary glory to the Father, the Son and the Holy Spirit, now and forever, and for ages of ages. Amen.[41]

Homily Five

On the verse of the prophet Isaiah that says, "In the year that King Uzziah died, I saw the Lord." And the proof that it was right for Uzziah to be struck with leprosy for offering incense without warrant, something permitted not to kings but to priests. [1]

Come now, today let us bring the story of Uzziah to an end and at this point cap off our treatment lest we be ridiculed, too, like the character in the Gospels who endeavored to build the tower but was unsuccessful, lest anyone present say also of us, "This fellow set out to build, but was not able to bring the job to completion." [2] For what has been said to be made clearer to you, however, (130) let us take up a little of what was previously said in case our treatment enter the spiritual theatre headless instead of adopting its proper appearance and being recognisable to the public. This will in fact serve two functions: as a reminder to those who heard it before, and as instruction to those who did not. The other day, then, we told how Uzziah had been pious but how he turned into a wretch, what was the cause of this, and the depths of arrogance to which he descended. Today instead we need to tell how he entered the sanctuary, how he endeavored to offer incense, how the priest opposed him, how he did not give way, how he brought down on himself God's wrath, how he ended his life in leprosy, and why the prophet passed over the days of his life and made mention of his death, speaking this way, "In the year that King Uzziah died." This was the reason, you see, that we covered the whole of the story from the outset. [3] Give careful attention, however.

"When King Uzziah grew strong, his heart was lifted up to the point of destruction, and he sinned against the Lord his God." What kind of sin? "He entered the Temple of the Lord to offer incense on the altar of incense." What awful presumption! what awful impudence! He violated the sacred precincts themselves, he burst into the Holy of Holies, a place out of bounds to all but the high priest – this he was bent on profaning.[4] Such is the condition of a soul once it despairs of its own salvation: instead of desisting from its frenzy, it surrenders the reins of its salvation to irrational desires and is carried about in all directions. Just as an untamed horse casts the bridle from its mouth, throws the rider from its back, moves in wilder fashion than any wind, and is resistant to anyone in its path, everyone getting out of its way and no one prepared to restrain it, so too a soul that casts away the fear of God restraining it and throws off the complete use of reason that reined it in betakes itself to the haunts of vice until it descends to the depths of ruin and jettisons its own salvation. Hence the need for it to be constantly held in check and to restrain its unreasoning impulses with thoughts of piety like some bridle – something Uzziah failed to do, infringing the very highest of all laws.

Priesthood, you see, is more exalted than kingship itself, and its responsibilities greater: do not quote me purple and diadem and golden robes – all of them shadows and of less substance than spring flowers. "All human glory is like the flower of grass,"[5] remember, even if you cite royal glory itself. Instead of citing me these things, however, if you want to see the difference between priest and king, examine the measure of authority given to each, and you will see the priest seated much higher than the king. I mean, even if the royal throne with the jewels attached to it and the gold encircling it strikes you as exalted, yet he has been chosen to administer the things of earth and has no authority beyond that, whereas the throne of priesthood is in (131) heaven and it has been entrusted with ordering things there. Who says so? The king of heaven himself: "Whatever you bind on earth will be bound in heaven, and whatever you loose on earth will be loosed in heaven."[6] What could be greater than this position? Heaven takes the cue for its judgement from earth. Since it is on earth that the judge is sitting, the master follows the slave; and whatever the latter decides here-below, he endorses on high. The priest has taken his place between God and human nature to bring honors down to us from there and take petitions from us up there, reconciling him to our common nature when he is angered, and rescuing us from his hands when we have given offence. Hence God even submits the royal head itself to the hands of the priest to teach us that the one ruler is more important than the other, the less being blessed by the greater, after all.

On the question of priesthood, however, and the greatness of its dignity we have made a statement at another time;[7] for the time being let us see the magnitude of the king's iniquity – or, rather, the tyrant's. He entered the Lord's Temple, and the priest Azariah entered behind him. Surely it was not without point that I said the priest is more important than the king? He entered with great determination, bent on driving him out not as king but as a fugitive and ungrateful slave, like some noble hound pursuing an unclean animal to hunt it from its master's house. Do you see a soul marked by great forthrightness and lofty attitude? His eyes were not on the importance of the office, he gave no thought to all that was involved in restraining a soul intoxicated with desire, he paid no heed to Solomon's words, "A king's threats are like a lion's rage."[8] Instead, with eyes on the real kingdom in heaven, his mind on that awesome tribunal and the account to be rendered, and gaining strength from these thoughts, he thus confronted the tyrant. He knew, of course, he clearly knew that a king's threats are like a lion's rage for those with eyes fixed on earth; but for someone imagining heaven and prepared to give up his life within the precincts rather than overlook the violation of the sacred laws, that man was more insignificant than any dog. Nothing, after all, is weaker than the transgressor of the divine laws, just as consequently nothing is stronger than the vindicator of the divine laws. "The one who commits sin," remember, "is a slave of sin,"[9] even if wearing countless crowns on his head, whereas the one who works for righteousness is more kingly than the king himself, even if the least of all.

Pondering this, that noble man accosted the king. So let us, too, as a body make our entrance, if you do not mind, so as to see what he says to the king. It is permissible, in fact: there are no slight grounds for gaining benefit from seeing a king reproved by a priest. So what does the priest say? "It is not permitted to you, Uzziah, to offer incense to the Lord."[10] He did not give him the title of king, nor refer to his office by name, since in anticipation he dismissed him from his position. Do you see a priest's forthrightness? Learn, then, his gentleness as well: we need not only forthrightness when we are due to reprove, but also gentleness to a greater extent than (132) forthrightness. I mean, since sinners abhor and hate no human being as much as the person bent on reproving them, and long to seize any opportunity to take to their heels and dodge the censure, it is therefore necessary to take hold of them with gentleness and moderation. A person of that kind, you see, will be a burden to sinners, not only by the tone of voice but also in appearance: "Even in appearance they are a burden to us."[11] Hence the need to display great gentleness; hence, too, the sermon has brought to your attention both the sinner and the one about to correct him.

The practitioners of medicine, after all, when about to amputate gangrenous limbs or extract stones lodged in the passages or correct any other fault of nature, do so not by taking the patients off into a corner but by placing them in the middle of the marketplace, and after forming the passers-by into a theatre they make the incision in that fashion. Now, they do this, not out of a wish to make a display of human misadventures, but for everyone to take great care of their own health. This is the way Scripture does things, too: when it makes an example of some sinner, it publicises them at the top of its voice, not in the middle of the marketplace but in the middle of the whole earth; by forming the world into a theatre it thus gives a display of its surgical skills to teach us to be more careful about our own salvation. So let us see how the priest proceeds to administer correction at this time. He did not say, O vilest of villains, you have overturned and confused everything, you have gone to the extremes of impiety; neither did he deliver his words of accusation at great length. Instead, just as the surgeons take trouble to perform their task briskly, disguising the sense of pain with the speed of the incision, so too this man lanced the king's inflammation with the brevity of his rebuke: like the knife in the case of the incisions, so was the reproof in the case of the sins.

He gives us evidence of moderation by his brevity in particular; but if you want to see as well the cutting edge of his words and how he disguised the blade, listen to this. "It is not permitted to you," the text says, "to offer incense to the Lord – only to the priests, the sons of Aaron, who are consecrated." Here he delivered the blow; how he did it I shall explain. Why, in fact, did he not say simply "the priests" instead of going on to mention Aaron? Because he was the first high priest and in his time a similar violation was committed. Dathan, Koran and Abiram, remember, rebelled against him, and along with some others tried to eject him from his office; but the earth opened up and swallowed some of them, and fire came down from on high and burnt up the others.[12] In his wish to remind him of this story, then, he referred him to the wrong done to Aaron at that time so as to direct his mind to the disaster that befell the wrongdoers. All to no avail, however – not through any fault of the priest but through the king's audacity. He should, in fact, have commended the priest and expressed gratitude for the advice; but he grew angry, the text says, and inflicted a worse wound, sin being not such an evil thing as effrontery after sin. (133)

This was not David's way, however. How did he react? After the accusation leveled at him by Nathan over Bathsheba, he responded, "I have sinned against the Lord."[13] Do you see a contrite heart? see a humbled spirit? see how splendid are even the falls of the saints? In other words, just as attractive bodies display many traces of charm even in ill-health, so too the souls of the saints even in their very faults show the signs of their distinctive virtue. Admittedly, in his case he was challenged by the prophet in the middle of the palace in the presence of many people, whereas this man was inside in the precincts when he received the reproof with no one as witness – and yet he still did not accept the reprimand. So what happened? did he remain incurable? Not at all, thanks to God's lovingkindness: just as in the case of the lunatic, when the disciples failed to drive out the demon, Christ said, "Bring him to me here,"[14] so too in this case, when the priest did not succeed in expelling the sin, an ailment worse than any demon, God himself then took the patient in hand. What did he do? He made leprosy break out on his forehead: "When he was threatening the priest," the text says, "leprosy broke out on his forehead."[15] He then left, and just as those being led off to their death carry the noose in their mouth as a sign of the verdict of condemnation, so too he carried a sign of dishonor on his forehead, no executioners leading him off, and instead leprosy in place of executioners pushing him head first.[16] He entered to take hold of priesthood, but he lost kingship; he entered to assume greater importance, but he fell further under a curse, an unclean person being then more despicable than any private citizen. Such is the evil of not keeping to the limits of the gifts given us by God, whether this concerns office or knowledge.[17] Have you not observed the sea, how it is irresistible in force, what great waves it builds up? Nevertheless, after rising to a great height and advancing with awful fury, its billows turn to foam once it reaches the limit imposed on it by God, and it returns to its own state – yet what could be more feeble than sand? That is not the obstacle, however: it is respect for the one who imposed it. Now, if this example does not bring you to your senses, take a lesson from what happened to Uzziah, as I have just told it to you.

After seeing God's wrath and the deserved retribution, however – come now, let us demonstrate also his lovingkindness and great moderation. I mean, we should direct attention not only to wrath but also to goodness in case we force the listeners to despair or to indifference. This is Paul's practice, also, tempering his exhortation with both of these attributes when he speaks this way, "Behold, then, the goodness and the severity of God," [18] so as to raise up the fallen both with fear and with sound hope. Do you see God's severity? See also his goodness. How, then, shall we see his goodness? If we learn what Uzziah deserved. (134) So what did he deserve? As soon as he made an assault on the sacred vestibule with such effrontery, he deserved countless thunderbolts and extreme punishment and retribution. After all, if those who were first guilty of this presumption paid this penalty, those in the company of Dathan, Korah and Abiram, much more should this man have been similarly punished for not learning the lesson even of their fate. God, however, did not do this; instead, he first applied words from the priest brimming with great moderation. What Christ also urged people to do when they sin against one another God did to this fellow; he said, remember, "When your brother sins against you, go, take the matter up with him between you and him alone." This was the way that God also took the matter up with the king: whereas Christ said, "If he does not listen to you, let him be like a pagan and a tax collector to you," [19] God in his lovingkindness surpassed his own laws in not felling him on the spot nor expelling him for resistance and anger, but making a further approach to him and teaching him a lesson by way of correction rather than retribution. I mean, instead of dispatching a thunderbolt from on high and consuming the shameless head by fire, he only taught him a lesson by leprosy.

Such is the story of Uzziah; but I have one further matter to raise, and shall then bring the sermon to a close. What is it? What we examined previously at the outset, why it is that in external affairs and in the inspired compositions everyone normally indicates the dates of the kings' life, whereas this author passed that over and makes mention of the time of his death, speaking this way, "In the year that King Uzziah died." Actually, the possibility was there to mention the dates of his reign, as all the inspired authors normally do; but he did not do it. Why, then, did he not do it? It was a law in ancient times for the leper to be driven out so that those in the city should enjoy better health, and that the leper not become the butt of jibes and jeers on the part of those inclined to offer abuse, but by staying outside the city have solitude as a veil over their affliction. This should have been the treatment of this king as well after his leprosy; but he was not so treated since those in the city respected him for his position, and instead he stayed secretly in his house. This provoked the Lord, this proved an obstacle to the charism of inspiration; and as was true in the case of Eli, "The word was precious, and there was no defining vision." [20]

Now, for your part, I ask you, consider God's lovingkindness: he did not overthrow the city or destroy its inhabitants; instead, what people do to those of their friends of equal standing by keeping their own counsel when they have some just cause for complaint against them God did towards this people who deserved a worse punishment and retribution. [21] While I expelled him from the sanctuary, he says, you did not expel him from the city; while I locked him in the bonds of leprosy and reduced him to a private citizen, you gained nothing from it and instead could not bring yourself to expel from the city the one condemned by me. What king in fact would take this mildly without completely overthrowing the city on seeing the one who had been ordered to be banished still living in the city? God did not do this, however: he was God, remember, not man.[22] But when he died, he brought to an end his anger towards the city along with the man's life, he opened the gates of inspiration and returned to them again.

You for your part, from the manner of reconciliation (135) consider God's lovingkindness: if one were to keep to the letter of the law, reconciling at that time would have been out of the question. Why? Because expulsion of Uzziah was no doing of theirs: instead of their seizing him and driving him out, it was by the law of nature that his end came upon him and finally expelled him. Far from being exact in these matters towards us, however, God looks for one thing only, a pretext for reconciliation with us. Let us be thankful to him for all this, let us glorify him for his ineffable lovingkindness. May it be the good fortune of us all to be proven worthy of this, thanks to the grace and mercy of his only-begotten Son, our Lord Jesus Christ, to whom with the Father and the Holy Spirit be glory, power and honor, now and forever, for ages of ages. Amen.

Homily Six

On the verse, "In the year King Uzziah died," and on repentance.[1]

We had difficulty negotiating the ocean on the subject of Uzziah, the difficulty in crossing it due not to the length of the journey but to the anxiety to learn on the part of you, our fellow navigators. This is the way also with a captain of a ship's company that is ambitious and desirous of visiting foreign cities: far from completing the voyage in one day, though it be only a day's journey, he is obliged to spend a longer time, daily tying up at every harbor, allowing a visit to every city so as to make some allowance for the interest of his fellow navigators.[2] This is what we did, too, not sailing by islands or giving a glimpse of harbors and ports and cities but upright men's virtue, sinners' indifference, a king's effrontery, a priest's forthrightness, God's wrath and lovingkindness, both of which were directed towards correction. Since, however, it is now the time to reach the point of entering the royal city, let us delay no longer, and instead keep ourselves in check as becomes those about to enter the city, and thus ascend to the mother city on high, the mother of us all, the free city,[3] where the seraphim are to be found, where the cherubim, where thousands of archangels, where tens of thousands of angels, where there is located the royal throne.

Therefore, let no one profane be in attendance, no one accurst: we are about to venture upon mystical doctrines. Let no one unclean or unworthy of hearing this be in attendance – or, rather, far from anyone profane or accurst being present, let them leave outside all uncleanness and wickedness, and then let them enter. The person with soiled garments, remember, the father of the bridegroom expelled from the bridal chamber and the inner sanctum for this reason, not for having soiled garments but for entering when wearing them. He did not say to them, you recall, Why do you not have a wedding garment, but "Why do you enter without a wedding garment?"[4] You have been standing on the street corners begging, and I was not put off by your poverty, I had no revulsion for your abject condition; instead, I rid you of all that lowliness and introduced you into the sacred bridal chamber, I regaled you with the royal banquet, and to dignity on high I led you, deserving though you were of extreme punishment. You for your part, however, (136) instead of profiting from the kindnesses, persisted in your habitual wickedness, bringing dishonor on the wedding, bringing dishonor on the bridegroom. Now begone, therefore, and pay the penalty owing for such awful insensitivity.

Accordingly, let each of us, too, be careful not to receive such a rebuke, and by casting off every thought unworthy of the spiritual teaching let us take our place at the sacred table. "In the year that King Uzziah died," the text says, "I saw the Lord seated on a lofty and exalted throne." How he saw I do not know: while the fact that he saw he mentioned, on the way he saw he kept silence; what he said I accept, into what he left unsaid I do not pry; what has been revealed I grasp, I do not busy myself with what remains concealed – the reason for its being concealed, after all. The explanation of the Scriptures is a golden robe, the warp of gold, the woof of gold; I do not attach to it a border of spiders' webs, conscious as I am of the limitations of my own reasonings. Scripture says, "Do not shift ancient boundaries which your fathers set in place."[5] It is not safe to move boundaries; so how shall we change what God has determined for us? Do you want to find out how he saw God? Turn prophet yourself. How could this be possible, you ask, for someone with a wife and the care of children? It is possible, if you are willing, dearly beloved: he too had a wife and was the father of two children, yet none of this was a obstacle to him. Marriage is no obstacle, in fact, on the way to heaven: were it an obstacle, and a wife likely to undermine us, God in creating her at the beginning would not have called her "helpmate."[6]

My intention, then, had been to say what is meant by God's being seated: that is a posture of bodies, whereas the divine is bodiless. My intention had been to say what is meant by God's throne: God is not contained by a throne, the divine being uncircumscribed. But I am afraid I might, by spending time on instruction in these matters, postpone paying the debt. In fact, I have been noticing everyone hankering after the seraphim, not today only, but also from the first day; hence my sermon will cut its way through the ideas in its path as through a multitude of people, and move quickly to comment on that subject. "The seraphim were in attendance around him,"[7] the text goes on. Behold the seraphim, whom you were all once longing to see; so feast your eyes on them and satisfy your longing, yet not with alarm or with mind over-anxious, as happens at the arrival of the emperor. In that case, of course, this is normal behavior: instead of the bodyguards waiting for the inspection of all onlookers, they force them to move along before everything has been properly seen by them. In this case, on the contrary, it is not like that: our sermon sets up the scene until you have taken it all in – to the extent that you are able to take it all in.

"The seraphim were in attendance around him." Before dealing with the dignity of their nature he taught us the dignity that comes from their nearness in position: instead of saying first what the seraphim were, he mentioned where they were standing, this dignity being higher than the other. How so? Because it shows that the importance of those powers was not so much in their being seraphim as in their standing near (137) the royal throne. We too, remember, class those bodyguards as more eminent whom we see riding near the royal chariot; likewise those incorporeal powers are also more conspicuous who are nearest the throne. Hence the prophet also neglected to mention the dignity of their nature and told us first of their pride of place, aware that this distinction is greater and that this is the ornament of their nature; this in fact is their glory, honor and utter security, their appearing around that throne.

This can be observed also in the case of the angels: wishing to bring out their greatness Christ also said, not that they are angels, about which he kept silence, but that "their angels constantly gaze upon the face of my Father in heaven:"[8] just as in that case gazing on the face of the Father is more important than the angelic dignity, so being in attendance around the throne and having it in their midst is more important than the seraphic dignity. This greatness, however, is possible also for you to receive if you are willing: he is in fact not in the midst of the seraphim only, but also of our very selves if we are willing. "Where two or three are gathered together in my name," Scripture says, remember, "there am I in the midst of them,"[9] and, "The Lord is close to the contrite of heart, and he will save the humble in spirit."[10] Hence Paul also cries aloud, "Direct your thoughts to what is above, where Christ is seated at the right hand of God."[11] Do you see how he puts us with the seraphim, bringing us close to the royal throne?

Then the text goes on, "Each with six wings." What do these six wings suggest to us? The loftiness, sublimity, lightness and celerity of those natures. Hence Gabriel also came down with wings, not that that incorporeal nature has wings, but that it left the highest regions and forsook its occupation up there to come here. Now, what is the number of the wings? There is no need of comment from us at this point: the text gives its own solution, explaining the need of them to us: "With two they covered their faces," and rightly so, as though protecting their eyes with some barrier on account of their inability to bear the rays emitted by that awesome glory. "With two they covered their feet," perhaps on account of their very astonishment:[12] we ourselves, when struck by some marvel, normally cover all parts of the body. Why mention the body when in fact even the soul itself on experiencing an extraordinary apparition shuts down its activities and retreats to its own depths, covering itself with the body like a kind of cloak. Let no one, however, on hearing of astonishment and marvel think some unpleasant trial had befallen them: coupled with this astonishment comes also an unbearable satisfaction. "With two they were flying:" this is a sign of their constant hankering for higher things and never looking below.

"They cried out to one another, (138) Holy, holy, holy."[13] The cry in turn is a very clear sign to us of their wonder:

instead of simply singing praise, they do it with a loud cry; and instead of simply with a cry, they also do it unceasingly. The most attractive human bodies, you see, even if extraordinarily attractive, normally astonish us only when they catch our attention for the first time, whereas when we have spent further time looking at them, we lose the sense of wonder through our eyes then becoming used to the bodies. This is the reason we are taken aback when we see also a royal image recently displayed, gleaming with the colors in which it is painted, but not beyond the first or second day.[14] Why mention a royal image when in fact we have the same experience from the very rays of the sun, than which no body could be more splendid; in like manner in the case of all bodies repetition dispels wonder. This is not the situation, however, with God's glory – quite the opposite: the more these powers occupy themselves with the contemplation of that wonderful glory, the more they are astonished and deepen the wonder. This is the reason, to be sure, that from the time of their creation up to their now viewing that wonderful glory, they never ceased crying out with astonishment; instead, what we experience for a short time when lightning flashes before our eyes they ceaselessly are subjected to, and without end they enjoy the marvel with a certain satisfaction. They not only cried out, note, but also did it to one another, a sign of their profound astonishment; we too likewise, when a thunderclap strikes or the earth is shaken, not only take fright and run around but also shout to one another. This what the seraphim did, too – hence their crying out one to the other, "Holy, holy, holy."

Do you not recognise this cry? is it from us or from the seraphim? It is both from us and from the seraphim on account of Christ's removal of the dividing wall and making peace between things in heaven and things on earth, on account of his making the two groups one.[15] At first, you see, this hymn was sung only in heaven; but when the Lord deigned to come on earth, he brought this music to us as well. Hence this great high priest, too, having taken his place at this holy table, offering the rational worship and performing the bloodless sacrifice, does not simply invite us to this praise-giving: having first mentioned the cherubim and recalled the seraphim, he then bids all offer up the awesome chant, urging us to lift our thoughts from earth to heaven by reference to our fellow choristers, and as it were crying out to each one of us in the words, You sing with the seraphim: take your place with the seraphim, with them spread the wings of your mind, with them fly around the royal throne. What is remarkable if you take your place with the seraphim when in fact God has readily granted to you what the seraphim do not presume to touch? "One of the seraphim was sent to me," the text goes on, remember, "with a burning coal which he had taken from the altar with a pair of tongs."[16] (139) That altar is a type and image of this altar, that fire of this spiritual fire. The seraphim, however, do not presume to touch by hand, only with a tongs, whereas you receive it in your hand.[17] I mean, if you look at the dignity of the offering, it is far beyond the touch of the seraphim, whereas if you consider the lovingkindness of the Lord, he is not ashamed to come down on the offering by his grace towards our lowliness.

Pondering this, therefore, mortal that you are, and considering the greatness of the gift, rise up, part company with the earth and ascend to heaven. But does the body drag you back and force you down? Behold, however, the approach of fasting,[18] which provides the soul with light wings while making the burden of the flesh light, even if finding a body heavier than any lead. Let our treatment of fasting wait its turn, however: now is the time for treatment of the sacraments to be undertaken, since even fasting is directed to them. I mean, just as in the Olympic games the crown is the goal of the contests, so too undefiled fellowship[19] is the goal of fasting; so unless we practise this in these days, it is idly and to no purpose that we torture ourselves, and we then take our leave uncrowned and bereft of the prizes from trials of fasting. This is the reason why our fathers also lengthened the course of fasting, giving us a determined period for penance so that having purified and cleansed ourselves we may then make our approach. This is the reason why I too here and now cry out with clear voice, I adjure, I beseech and implore that you not approach this sacred table with a stain, with a bad conscience; that would be no profit, nor would it be fellowship, even if times beyond number we were to touch that holy body – only condemnation and punishment and additional retribution.

So let no sinner approach the table – or, rather, I do not say, No sinner, since I would be the first to be excluded from the divine table; instead, let no one continuing in sin approach. Hence I here and now give prior warning in case anyone should be in a position to say, when the royal banquet and the sacred vigil arrive,[20] I entered here unprepared and am excluded, this warning should have been given earlier; in fact, if I had heard it earlier, I would have been completely changed, I would have purified myself completely before entering. Lest, then, anyone be in a position to make this excuse, I here and now adjure you ahead of time and urge you to give evidence of fervent repentance. I know that we are all worthy of chastisement, and that no one will boast of having a pure heart; the problem, however, is not that we do not have a pure heart but that, though not having a pure heart, we do not approach the one who can make it pure. He can if he wishes, in fact, and he wishes more than we ourselves; but he waits to get some slight excuse from us for crowning us with certainty. Who could be more sinful than the tax collector? Yet because he said only, "Be merciful to me a sinner,"[21] he went down justified to a greater extent than the pharisee.

What, in fact, was the great efficacy of that expression? It was not the expression that purified him, however, but the disposition with which he uttered the expression (140) – or, rather, not only the disposition but God's lovingkindness before it. I mean, what sort of good deed, tell me, what sort of effort, what sort of exertion on the sinner's part could persuade him that he is a sinner? Do you see that it was not without purpose that I said he wishes to derive some slight excuse from us, and for his part he contributes everything to our salvation?[22] Let us therefore repent, let us weep, let us lament. Frequently when someone loses a daughter, they spend much of their life grieving and lamenting: for our part do we lose our soul and not lament? do we forfeit salvation and not bewail it? Why mention soul and salvation? have we not provoked a Lord so gentle and mild and have not buried ourselves underground? In his care for us, after all, he surpasses all the benevolence not only of a caring lord but also of a loving father and an affectionate mother. "Would a woman forget her baby," Scripture says, "so as not to take pity on the issue of her womb? But even if a woman did forget, I would not forget you, says the Lord."[23] While the declaration, then, is reliable even before proof, being from God, yet come now, let us provide proof even from past events. Once upon a time Rebekah bade her son play a role in the theft of the blessings, dressing him up nicely in every respect and giving him the appearance of his brother; but when she saw that even so he lacked confidence, in her wish to remove all apprehension from her son she said, "Your curse be upon me, child."[24] Truly the statement of a mother on fire with love for her son. Christ, however, not only said this but also put it into practice; he not only made a promise but also proved it in action. Paul cries out in the words, "Christ redeemed us from the curse of the Law, becoming a curse for us."[25] Shall we, therefore, I ask you, provoke him? how would this not be worse than hell itself, the undying worm, the unquenchable fire?[26]

When you are about to approach the sacred table, therefore, reflect that the king of all things is also present there: he is really present, knowing the disposition of each person, and he sees who approaches with due holiness and who with a bad conscience, with impure and filthy thoughts, with disgusting actions. If he were to find someone in that condition, for the time being he would leave them to the tribunal of conscience; then if they took themselves in hand, chastised themselves in thought and made themselves better, God would admit them in due course. But if they remain unreformed, he orders the insensitive ingrate to be given into his hands. "It is a fearful thing to fall into the hands of the living God."[27] I realise the words are biting – but what am I to do? Were I not to apply harsh remedies, the wound would not disappear; were I to apply harsh remedies, you would not bear the pain. (141) I am under pressure from both directions; but I must check my hand, my words being sufficient for the correction of those who are attentive.

For the words to be useful, however, not only to you but also to others through you – come now, let us sum up once more. We discoursed of the seraphim, we showed how great their dignity in standing close to the royal throne and the fact that this dignity can be attained also by human beings. We spoke about the wings and God's unapproachable power, and about his considerateness in our regard.[28] We went on to the cause of their loud cry and unceasing wonder, and how in unceasing contemplation the praise of the seraphim is also unceasing. We reminded you of the kind of choir we joined and of those with whom we sang the praises of the common Lord. We had further words to say about repentance; and finally we demonstrated the terrible evil it is to approach the sacraments with a bad conscience, and (142) how there is no escape for the one who is guilty of such things.[29]

Let a wife also come to know this from her husband, a

child from its father, a servant from a master, neighbor from neighbor, friend from friend [30] – or, rather, let us speak of this also to our enemies: we are accountable for their salvation as well. After all, if we are bidden to pick up their beasts that have fallen and rescue and recover those that have gone astray, [31] much more should we recover their soul when it is gone astray and raise it up when fallen. If we conduct in this way our own affairs and those of the neighbor, we shall be able with confidence to stand before the judgement seat of Christ, [32] to whom with the Father and the holy and life-giving Spirit be glory, honor and might, now and forever, for ages of ages. Amen.

Select Bibliography

Aubineau, M., "Restitution de quatorze folios du codex hierosolymitain, Photios 47, au codex Saint-Sabas 32. Prédications de Chrysostome à Constantinople et notamment à Saint-Irène," *JThS* 43 (1992) 528-44

Augustin, P., "La pérennité de l'´Eglise selon St. Jean Chrysostome et l'authenticité de la IVe Homélie 'Sur Ozias'," *Recherches Augustiniennes* 28 (1995) 95-144

Barthélemy, D., *Les Devanciers d'Aquila*, VTS X, Leiden, 1963

Baur, P. C., *John Chrysostom and his Time*, 2 vols, Eng. trans., London-Glasgow, 1959,1960

Bouyer, L., *The Spirituality of the New Testament and the Fathers*, Eng. trans., London, 1963

Drewery, B., "Antiochien," *TRE* 3, 103-113

Dumortier, J., *Jean Chrysostome. Homélies sur Ozias*, SC 277, Paris, 1981

_____ , *Jean Chrysostome. Commentaire sur Isaïe*, SC 304, Paris, 249

Fernandez Marcos, N., "Some reflections on the Antiochian text of the Septuagint," in D. Fraenkel et al (edd.), *Studien zur Septuaginta – Robert Hanhart zu Ehren*, Göttingen, 1990, 219-229

_____ , "The Lucianic text in the Books of Kingdoms," in A. Pietersma et al (edd.), *De Septuaginta*, Mississauga, 1984

_____ , *The Septuagint in Context: Introduction to the Greek Versions of the Bible*, Eng. trans., Boston-Leiden, 2001

Hill, R. C., "St. John Chrysostom's teaching on inspiration in 'Six Homilies on Isaiah'," *VC* 22 (1968) 19-37

_____ ,"*Akribeia*: a principle of Chrysostom's exegesis," *Colloquium* 14 (Oct. 1981) 32-36

_____ , "Chrysostom's terminology for the inspired Word," *EstBíb* 41 1983) 367-73

_____ , *St. John Chrysostom's Homilies on Genesis*, FOTC

74,82,87, 1986, 1990, 1992

_____, "Psalm 45: a *locus classicus* for patristic thinking on biblical inspiration," *StudP* 25 (1991) 95-100

_____, "Chrysostom's Commentary on the Psalms: homilies or tracts?" in P. Allen et al (edd.), *Prayer and Spirituality in the Early Church* I, Brisbane 1998

_____, "A pelagian commentator on the Psalms?" *ITQ* 65 (1998) 263-71

_____, *St. John Chrysostom. Commentary on the Psalms*, 2 vols, Brookline MA, 1998

_____, "Chrysostom's homilies on David and Saul," *SVTQ* 44 (2000) 123-41

_____, "St. John Chrysostom's homilies on Hannah," *SVTQ* 45 (2001) 319-38

_____, "St. John Chrysostom's Six Homilies on Isaiah 6," *SVTQ*

_____, "Chrysostom on the obscurity of the Old Testament," *OCP* 67 (2001) 371-83

Kelly, J. N. D., *Early Christian Doctrines*, 5th ed., New York, 1978

_____, *Golden Mouth. The Story of John Chrysostom. Ascetic, Preacher, Bishop*, Ithaca NY, 1995

Leroux, J.-M., "Johannes Chrysostomus," *TRE* 17, 118-27

Mayer, W., Allen, P., *John Chrysostom*, The Early Church Fathers, London-New York, 2000

Schäublin, C., "Diodor von Tarsus," *TRE* 8, 763-67

_____, *Untersuchungen zu Methode und Herkunft der Antiochenischen Exegese*, Theophaneia: Beiträge zur Religions- und Kirchengeschichte des Altertums 23, Köln-Bonn, 1974

Ternant, P., "La θεωρία d'Antioche dans le cadre de sens de l''Ecriture," *Bib* 34 (1953) 135-58,354-383,456-86

Vaccari, A., "La θεωρία nella scuola esegetica di Antiochia," *Bib* 1 (1920) 3-36

von Rad, G., *Studies in Deuteronomy*, Studies in Biblical Theology 9, London, 1963

Wallace-Hadrill, D. S., *Christian Antioch. A Study of Early Christian Thought in the East*, Cambridge, 1982

Young, F., *Biblical Exegesis and the Formation of Christian Culture*, Cambridge, 1997.

Notes

Notes to the Homily on Jeremiah

[1] Chrysostom, who can both lament his congregations' lack of biblical literacy and flatter them with the ability to decide on difficult matters of interpretation, speaks here like a teacher choosing a range of topics during a sustained and carefully planned program. Yet, as noted above, the text for the day's homily seems to have been determined for the preacher by the liturgy (he speaks of the Jer text as being "read out"). The text of the homily, edited in the eighteenth century by Bernard de Montfaucon, is found in PG 56.153-62 (nos. incorporated into the translation for convenient reference). For a more lengthy study of this homily, see my article, "'Norms, definitions, and unalterable doctrines:' Chrysostom on Jeremiah." ITQ [ital.] 65 (2000) 335-46.

[2] Cf Gal 2.11; Acts 11.19-26. Paul, Chrysostom's beau ideal, is mentioned ahead of Peter (though his views are about to be contested). Origen had initiated the idea that the dispute was only a "pious pretence," in Montfaucon's phrase, and Jerome concurred; Augustine would have none of it.

[3] Eustathius was a bishop of Antioch, prominent at the Council of Nicea, who was much persecuted by the Arians and later abdicated or was deposed. Mention of these previous homilies encourages Montfaucon to place the Jeremiah homily also in Antioch. Dom Baur, Chrysostom's biographer, would take references such as these to audience reaction as "appearances of actuality" confirming oral delivery of the material by contrast with written composition; but it is not unknown for such signs of spontaneity to be manufactured.

[4] Montfaucon observes that imagery from pugilistic contests would appeal to Chrysostom's Antioch audience.

[5] Cf Gal 5.22. Chrysostom, great rationalizer that he is, is anxious to dissipate an impression of hostility between the apostles.

[6] It is axiomatic in Antiochene theology and spiritual direction that human effort has at least as important a role to play in the process of salvation as divine grace. Hence the value of zeal and enthusiasm, προθυμία, and the harm in indifference, ῥᾳθυμία. Insistence on this led to charges of pelagianism against some members of the school of Antioch; see my "A pelagian commentator on the Psalms?" in reference to Chrysostom. So he cannot afford to allow a lax attitude based on this Jeremiah text, or similar ones like Rom 9.16 or Ps 127.1, to gain credence; it is, he claims, tantamount to cutting the anchor and sinking the ship.

⁷ For an Antiochene commentator, the required response to loose citation of scriptural texts in support of aberrant positions is ἀκρίβεια, precision in approach.

⁸ The divine inspiration of the biblical authors is a given; as Chrysostom says in his commentary on Isa 6 below, "The mouths of the inspired authors are the mouth of God."

⁹ This commendable exegetical principle is exactly the approach Chrysostom needed to apply later in Constantinople in wrestling with Isa 45.6-7, which did not yield to a less thorough study in isolation without reference to the wider context. Physician, heal thyself.

¹⁰ Ps 14.1.

¹¹ Ps 10.11,13.

¹² 1 Cor 7.8-9.

¹³ 1 Tim 5.11-12.

¹⁴ We continue to get formal lessons on interpretation in place of examination of the Jeremiah text quoted. Sound as they are, and at variance with the preacher's own practice at times, they strike us as unusually bookish for a homily to a normal congregation.

¹⁵ Hag 2.8.

¹⁶ Gen 1.26. In the long lecture on the dangers of misinterpretation of Scripture, the day's text has been lost from sight. The preacher needs to remind himself of that danger as well; and in fact Chrysostom shortly returns to the day's text.

¹⁷ Cf Jer 7.16.

¹⁸ Jer 10.24. Chrysostom commendably sets about applying his principles of interpretation to the verse in question, first situating it in its historical context. Prophetic oracles, especially of Jeremiah, however, are notoriously resistant to precision about dating and situation, as Chrysostom finds in being confronted with different views. Unlike some modern (and ancient) commentators, who would see 10.23 as a proverbial axiom coming from the prophet's ministry under Jehoiakim, Chrysostom chooses to give it an historical reference to Babylonian incursions, which occurred later in the period of Zedekiah.

¹⁹ Cf Jer 10.19-22.

²⁰ As observed above in note 6, the common misunderstanding of the Jeremiah verse is lamented by Chrysostom particularly as it directly undermines Antiochene morality, which rests on a balance between the roles of divine grace and human effort in the process of salvation. In their efforts to correct the misunderstanding and offset ῥαθυμία, the Antiochenes can frequently seem to shift the balance in the other direction; we shall see Chrysostom not escaping this tendency here.

²¹ Cf Luke 18.10-14.

²² Matt 20.6-7.

²³ If human effort and enthusiasm have an essential role in salvation, *a priori* human independence and free will must be preserved. Chrysostom has to insist on this.

[24] Matt 23.37. In the Antiochene view of the economy of salvation, God cooperates with us, not we with God.

[25] The LXX text of Sir 2.10 refers to a person remaining faithful to "his fear;" Chrysostom may be loosely recalling this, or adjusting it to his purpose. Montfaucon observes, "Chrysostom is accustomed to apply these texts as they come to mind."

[26] Rom 5.5.

[27] 1 Cor 10.13.

[28] Sir 1.1-2.

[29] Matt 10.22.

[30] Luke 22.31-32.

[31] Cf John 6.66.

[32] Cf Acts 10.34-35.

[33] Isa 1.19-20.

[34] Finally Chrysostom comes clean on what are Antioch's "norms, definitions and unalterable doctrines." Paul, though at first quoted in support, is now contradicted: willing and acting are up to us, and in fact are means of bringing God around to do his part so that we succeed in achieving our goal. The popular misinterpretation of the Jeremiah verse was clearly at the other extreme, and had to be rebutted.

Notes to Homilies on Isaiah

[1] PG 56.141-42. That ms, which Montfaucon admits is faulty and in need of emendation, is Bayerische Staatsbibliotek gr.6, according to M. Aubineau, "Restitution de quatorze folios du codex hierosolymitain, Photios 47, au codex Saint-Sabas 32. Prédications de Chrysostome à Constantinople et notamment à Sainte-Irène," *JThS* 43 (1992) 534. The title given by the Jerusalem codex to this homily identifies Constantinople as place of delivery, as do other mss in Rome and Florence.

[2] This sense of the word emerges in Chrysostom's commentary on some other psalms; see the Introduction to my translation, *St. John Chrysostom. Commentary on the Psalms*, 10. The Latin version of the Isaiah homily by Fronto de Duc in PG 56 misses this sense in rendering the word as *obedientia*.

[3] Diodore is credited with formulations of Antioch's preference for the literal sense of the scriptural text, which also included recognition of forms of expression such as irony and paradox; to fail to recognize them would mean moving from the literal to a literalist interpretation, and Chrysostom has shown (as in his Psalms Commentary) he is aware of the difference.

Notes to Isaiah 45:6-7

[1] Text is found in PG 56.143-52.

[2] As in Antioch, so in Constantinople Chrysostom finds his bête noire, the people's proclivity to desert his synaxeis for the races. For those attending he is going to discourse fully on the text after the former speaker

used it (or perhaps the opening verses of Ps 137, the day's psalm: cf note 28) simply as a responsorium, ὑπακοή, sung by the congregation.

[3] "He means the Manichees," editor Montfaucon notes. Even if Chrysostom can at times, like many a preacher, deliver himself of an otherworldly remark unhelpful for his congregation living in the world, he is no dualist.

[4] Ps 104.24. The verse from Isaiah, evidently forming part at least of the first reading of the liturgy of the Word for the day (in addition to Pauline and Gospel readings, as emerges below), is immediately forgotten and a digression entered into stemming from the preacher's insistence on the goodness of creation that dualists impugn. The resulting disproportion in the homily is an index of the orality of the material; a desk theologian would surely keep the central text in view.

[5] Ps 19.1. If we were to place this homily early in Chrysostom's ministry, we might say that the rather lengthy commentary that Chrysostom now conducts on the opening verses of this psalm could explain why it does not figure among the fifty-eight psalms appearing in his formal Commentary; other psalms, such as Ps 42, have received similar treatment. But in the Introduction to my translation of that Commentary I have presented signs of early immaturity in that work, just as a Psalms commentary was Theodore's first exegetical work and Theodoret intended his to be. In any case, Aubineau's case for a date for this homily no earlier than February 398, the time of Chrysostom's consecration in Constantinople, is cogent.

[6] Ps 19.2-3. For an Antiochene theologian like Chrysostom, who is no dualist, the παχύτης of scriptural statement (as also of the humanity of Jesus) is not to be despised; but people of an overly materialistic mentality (παχύτεροι) are in danger of misinterpreting anthropomorphic statements found in the Scriptures, as he will repeatedly remind them.

[7] Also typical of an Antiochene commentator is attention to details in the text: the precision, ἀκρίβεια, of the text requires a like precision in the commentator.

[8] Matt 5.16.

[9] It has indeed been a lengthy and rather repetitive digression directed at dualist deprecation of the goodness of creation, as observed in note 4. Is the preacher by such a stratagem trying to forestall having to come to grips with a difficult text? The "alarm" prompted by the text that he detects in his congregation may be a projection of his own feeling of inadequacy before it.

[10] Chrysostom can imply some scriptural illiteracy in his congregations, and at the same time flatter them with the ability to decide moot points of interpretation.

[11] Matt 9.20-22, the Gospel reading for the day, preceded (at least at this stage in byzantine liturgies) by an Old Testament reading (in this case Isaiah 45.6-7 – chosen, as in western liturgies today, to background the Gospel text?) and another, non-evangelical New Testament reading (in this case, evidently from 2 Cor 6 or 11, which also could be seen relating to

the Gospel). See note 28 regarding the day's responsorial psalm.

[12] Chrysostom is loosely recalling Paul's lists of hardships suffered that occur in 2 Cor 6.4-5 and 11.23-27, whichever was the reading for the day. He goes on to admit his affinity with the apostle (and especially his undeserved hardships?), which emerges in his other works.

[13] A phrase frequently in the mouth of Antiochene commentators like Chrysostom and Theodoret, whose motto in commentary is "Take nothing for granted: every detail is significant." It is the principle of ἀκρίβεια, and applies, of course, beyond scriptural commentary to Christology and soteriology.

[14] Amos 3.6. There is a paradox in the two Isaian verses, clearly, and the reason for the preacher's delay in resolving the paradox (which perhaps the inspired authors did not want resolved, that being the point of their statement) may lie in the inherent difficulty, for which rationalizing may prove to be the only – and customary – solution. But at least his hermeneutical principle, "Learn the force of the expressions," is sound, and typically Antiochene: language must be grasped at the literal level, which includes acknowledgement of the figures employed by the composer, such as paradox. Only thus can you "depth the meaning," as he says.

[15] Chrysostom in his time cannot speak of poverty as a social, structural problem for which there are strategies of eradication to be adopted; so, as in commenting on Ps 4.7, where he declares that "poverty is the mother of wisdom," he falls again to rationalizing it as a trick of fate like skin color or state of health, and to recommending almsgiving while berating the rich for vulgar display of their riches.

[16] Job 1.21 LXX. As is often the case with preachers, Chrysostom is selective in his reading of this book, referring only to its prose framework and ignoring the cursing Job of the verse dialogue.

[17] Job 31.32.

[18] Prov 9.9.

[19] 1 Tim 5.23.

[20] Does Chrysostom have Tobit in mind?

[21] 2 Thess 3.10.

[22] Phil 1.22-24.

[23] Pss 116.15; 34.21 LXX.

[24] This seems a particularly loose recall of two verses of Eccl 3, neither (4,2) referring thus to life and death. The author's fatalistic theme in this poem, of course, does not support Chrysostom's point that it is our attitude, γνώμη, that is the deciding factor.

[25] 2 Cor 7.10.

[26] Phil 4.4. The paradox of the Isaian verse is leading Chrysostom almost to the point of declaring that black is white so as to acquit God of the charge of being responsible for evil, instead of seeking a clue in the wider context of Second Isaiah.

[27] 1 Kgs 17.1. For Chrysostom indifference, ῥᾳθυμία, is the basic flaw, cause of the sin of the first parents.

[28] Cf Ps 137.1-3. Is this psalm that they "are obliged to focus on today" the responsorial psalm in the day's liturgy?

[29] For the loud resonance of the prophetic denunciation Chrysostom employs the verb ἐνηχεῖν that he frequently uses elsewhere for the inspiration of the biblical authors by the Spirit, the verb having the meaning also of "ring in the ears." See my "Chrysostom's terminology for the inspired Word."

[30] We thus reach the end of the second protracted digression in the homily, like the first (see note 9) perhaps conducted as a deliberate ploy to avoid coming to grips with the paradox in the day's Old Testament reading, which even rationalizing is unsuccessful in resolving. The treatment has also, like the former digression, been anything but concise; does its repetitive character suggest the effect of age in the preacher?

[31] Cf Jonah 3.4.

[32] Jer 6.14 LXX.

[33] Chrysostom rarely gives credit to the scholars (here φιλόλογοι, elsewhere φιλομαθεῖς or φιλοπονώτεροι). The text of the rest of this sentence is corrupt, Montfaucon believes.

[34] Amos 3.6. For Chrysostom predictably, as one so respectful of divine transcendence, the paradox in the Isaian verse lies in attributing evil to God. He can only look for similar statements in the Scriptures, not seeking a solution (as do modern scholars) in the structure of these chapters of Second Isaiah, their purpose in the commissioning of Cyrus, and the inclusion linking 45.7 with 44.24, where similar key words are found.

[35] Matt 6.34.

[36] This is the classic Antiochene style of commentary, of course: apply ἀκρίβεια in studying each item of the text. Unfortunately, in a case like this, as we noted above, the clue lies in taking a wider rather than a narrower perspective; twisting words to mean something else will not resolve the paradox.

[37] So, in the end, after much rationalizing in an attempt to resolve a paradox that is particularly challenging for one imbued with a sense of divine transcendence, Chrysostom settles for a moralizing conclusion to the Isaian verse: misfortune can be converted into gain, as biblical examples demonstrate.

Notes to Homilies on Isaiah 6

[1] SC 277.90.
[2] SC 277.88.

Homily One

[1] Isa 6.1. For evidence that this homily is not the first in the series, see Introduction. Bernard de Montfaucon's eighteenth century edition of the text of the homilies (*In Illud: Vidi Dominum*; cf CPG 4417) is reprinted in

PG 56.95-142; a critical text has been edited by Jean Dumortier, *Homélies sur Ozias*. For a detailed study of the homilies, see my article, "St. John Chrysostom's Six Homilies on Isaiah."

[2] Particularly in view of the unlikely delivery of this homily as the first in the series, the recent occasion Chrysostom here refers to as πρώην is uncertain, as is also the content.

[3] The analogy of the farmer reaping an abundant harvest is a conventional one for a homilist, of course.

[4] Unless he has to chastise his congregation for irregular attendance or patronage of less edifying pastimes, Chrysostom can give a glowing account of their participation by way of indirect exhortation. This may be expressed more prosaically as a reference to assistance at a eucharistic synaxis in the evening, perhaps in Antioch's Old Church; the music may not have reached angelic heights, though elsewhere Chrysostom will speak of the congregation's response, ὑπακοή, as a sung responsorium. Actually, as with many a preacher, after the compliments Chrysostom has some bones to pick with his congregation about their behavior in church.

[5] In this trinitarian picture of heaven and earth joining together, Chrysostom sees as one element the Lord's συγκατάβασις, divine considerateness, which he will elsewhere apply to the concreteness, παχύτης, of biblical language. As with the biblical authors, the congregation are said to be inspired (the verb ενηχεῖν, Chrysostom's normal term for the process, occurring here, together with another conventional – if limited – analogy, a musician plucking an instrument). See my article, "St. John Chrysostom's teaching on inspiration in 'Six homilies on Isaiah'".

[6] Matt 11.28.

[7] Attendance at spectacles by fun-loving Antiochenes frequently meets with Chrysostom's ire. For them to introduce such depraved behavior into the liturgy was adding insult to injury. He obviously sees it as no mere pentecostalist fervor. It reminds Dumortier of whirling dervishes, but he recalls the censure of overly exuberant Christians in the early Church in 1 Cor 14.

[8] Chrysostom's church did not have a specific sacrament of reconciliation distinct from baptism, and yet unlike Novatian rigorism it did allow for forgiveness of sin committed later. Here he describes elements of such a rite within celebration of the eucharist, including recitation of Ps 51, not unlike a modern pentitential rite complete with *Kyrie eleison*.

[9] Ps 2.11 LXX.

[10] For eastern theologians like Chrysostom, kataphatic prying into the incomprehensible is anathema.

[11] A form of Isa 6.3 resembling the liturgical eucharistic text more than the biblical one.

[12] An obvious question for an Antiochene commentator, who scrutinizes the biblical text for its ἀκρίβεια.

[13] Isa 6.2 LXX.

[14] Chrysostom seems to have missed the euphemism intended, like the

one in 7.20 in the commentary on the eight chapters of Isaiah. So the reference to feet continues to intrigue him (he gives a different interpretation in Homily Six), and like a good Antiochene he will not let the detail escape. It is also true that mention of parts of the body suits his preoccupation with bodily movements in church.

[15] While some will observe that joined hands was not the normal posture for prayer in the east, Chrysostom is certainly unhappy with wild gesturing, as he will go on to insist. At the close he will repeat the direction for hands to be joined together, not waved about.

[16] Having approached the verse from the preferred Antiochene viewpoint of its literal sense, Chrysostom can now proceed to find a fuller sense, θεωρία, by a process of discernment, θεωρεῖν.

[17] Ps 51.17.

[18] Ps 66.1.

[19] The synaxis at which this homily was delivered is clearly a eucharistic one, comprising Word and sacrifice.

[20] Cf Matt 25.31-46.

[21] Historians like Tillemont and editor Montfaucon agree that the reference must be to conditions in the empire under Arcadius, who acceded to the throne in 395 – confirmation of this homily's being later than the following ones.

[22] Montfaucon would like to read "a person more righteous" here; but the weight of ms evidence is against such a reading.

[23] Chrysostom may be referring to the bishop of Constantinople, Nectarius, whom he was to succeed at his death in 397 – in which case the homily was delivered in Antioch.

[24] Cf Jas 5.16.

[25] Deut 7.3-4 certainly allows for such a scenario; Chrysostom sees it as a fact.

[26] Chrysostom can speak of his congregation as hardly biblically literate, and at other times flatter them with the ability to decide on moot points of biblical interpretation.

[27] Typology is an exercise an Antiochene feels encouraged to embark upon when encouraged by the New Testament, such as in this case the author of Hebrews (cf 4.8). As a pastor he can also give a text a sacramental dimension.

[28] Cf Jos 6.17-18.

[29] Jos 7.1.

[30] Jos 7.2,4,5.

[31] Ezek 18; Sir 23.11; John 8.21.

[32] Cf Jos 7.10-12.

[33] Cf Jos.7.20-21 LXX.

[34] Cf Jos 7.24-25. The story of Achan, documenting Chrysostom's thesis of a people's sin – even an individual's – bringing disaster on the whole commonwealth, has loomed larger than the Isaiah verses, doubtless owing to the current political situation that is on the preacher's mind.

[35] It is surely drawing the longbow to equate community responsibility for national disaster, as exemplified by Achan's sin, with lack of orderliness in worship. Chrysostom would not be the first preacher to adopt a fire-and-brimstone approach to parenesis, even where relatively trivial matters are involved.

[36] Isa 66.2 – another context in which more serious "abominations" are under fire.

[37] The homily, then, has not been prompted by a day's scriptural text. Rather, the preacher is concerned at lack of due decorum in church on the part of some of the congregation, and has first enlisted the Isaian passage as an example of angelic behavior in worship; then, blowing the indiscretions up out of all proportion, he has suggested such behavior is even responsible for recent national disasters, citing the example of Achan's violation of the ban in the book of Joshua as a (hardly credible) parallel.

Homily Two

[1] Isa 6.1.

[2] Not only does Chrysostom impress as a communicator with the apposite images he devises; he also shows he is not out of touch with the real life of his congregation (male though they may be). Cf also Gal 4.19; 1 Thess 2.7.

[3] Cf Matt 25.14-30. Though Chrysostom applies the principle here to his preaching, "making our contribution" is something he insists on in the spiritual life generally.

[4] Chrysostom here is clearly not referring to Homily One as the occasion πρώην; but it is not clear which "mystical" psalm (or "angelic" in some mss) was then "read out" – probably Ps 148, which however makes no mention of expelling sinners, though in his commentary on that psalm elsewhere he does stress the fact that not the whole human race but only "his holy ones" (v.14) may join in praise.

[5] This notion of the faculty of sight acting like a beam from a torch is that found in Plato and Theophrastus, Dumortier tells us.

[6] A dramatic presentation of the need for reverence in worship, unlike the fire-and-brimstone approach adopted in Homily One. The listeners must be on the edge of their seats – or, more accurately, holding their breath – as the scene develops.

[7] One of Chrysostom's more striking formulas for the belief in divine inspiration of the Scriptures and the divine revelation contained in them – conveyed to the congregation by the public reading of the text (and, Chrysostom would add, the commentary upon it).

[8] Isa 6.2-3.

[9] This notion of συγκατάβασις, considerateness (not "condescension," a common rendering that carries a patronizing connotation that is not intended), Chrysostom sees realized in both sacred Scripture and sacred history where God makes allowance for human (and here angelic) limitations.

[10] Chrysostom, with typical Antiochene resistance to kataphatic theology, is repulsed by Anomean claims that God's essence is comprehensible, directing homilies at various times in his life against the claim.

[11] Is Chrysostom comparing the Eunomians with the earlier, less radical Arians? Or with pagans?

[12] Dan 10.8-9.

[13] Again a classic Antiochene statement of belief in the inspiration of the Scriptures and the revelation they contain, together with the consequent precision, ἀκρίβεια, required of the reader – all conveyed by a most apposite analogy of mining for gold. "Not idly or to no purpose" is one oft-recurring slogan for this approach to the text. The statement on inspiration is applicable to all the inspired authors, προφῆται, not just a (Latter) prophet like Isaiah.

[14] Ps 12.6. Dumortier excludes the first half of the quotation from his text.

[15] It is not often Chrysostom speaks of the Bible *reader*. The analogy of the miner led him to think in terms of dipping into a book.

[16] For Chrysostom, Christians have rightly reclaimed Old Testament scriptures and characters.

[17] The limit case in the Antiochene position on the precision of Scripture, the significance of syllables and particles (Chrysostom likewise making capital of the "but" in Gen 2.20 in his homily on that passage). His precarious semitic background does not allow him to get beyond the popular etymology in Gen 17.5 that sees a meaning "father of a multitude" in Abraham, which in fact is simply a dialectal variant of Abram (which probably means "the father is exalted"). Theology, not linguistics, is Chrysostom's strongpoint.

[18] Chrysostom often displays an acquaintance with commercial life, as also with family life, we noted.

[19] Here Chrysostom is using προφητεία specifically of prophecy. In its wider sense of inspired (OT) composition generally, he can be quoted for essential characteristics other than accuracy in forecasting the future; for instance, in the second homily on the obscurity of the OT we shall see him declaring its essential purpose is for the listeners to reform their lives, and elsewhere too he stresses its moral and hagiographical purpose.

[20] Gen 49.10.

[21] John 5.43. Mention of Jewish shortcomings never fails to prompt Chrysostom to expatiate.

[22] Eccl 3.7. It has been a relatively short homily, for two reasons: Chrysostom is at the point of beginning the story of Uzziah's sacrilege, and the bishop (διδάσκαλος) is to exercise his role of speaking second.

[23] John 2.10. Chrysostom could not be accused of lacking in respect for Flavian, his bishop in Antioch. As well as outright flattery, he comes up also with some of his most apposite images in giving place in the pulpit; their particular inventiveness in this homily may be due to the bishop's presence.

Homily Three

[1] 2 Chr 26.16. This synopsis is somewhat astray in suggesting humility receives much attention in the homily; Chrysostom's own summary at the close is more accurate.

[2] Chrysostom speaks of the martyrs as having suffered in the lifetime of his congregation, whereas Dumortier thinks the reference is to the persecution under Diocletian.

[3] Flavian as bishop will speak second in the day's liturgy. Chrysostom spoke of Antioch's martyrs on other occasions.

[4] With a show of humility Chrysostom apologizes for the poverty of his offering (in a typically figurative opening); but in fact he was prevented from presenting Uzziah's story in the previous homily by the bishop's being present on that occasion also. Even on this occasion, however, he shows a reluctance to stay with the Uzziah story, and in fact he does spend much time on the historical details he now promises.

[5] Cf 2 Chr 26.15-16.

[6] Luke 17.10.

[7] Cf Isa 43.26.

[8] Some mss add "and confession" at this point, and Montfaucon includes the phrase.

[9] Sir 7.5, Chrysostom wittingly or unwittingly attributing this Wisdom book also to Solomon.

[10] 2 Chr 26.19.

[11] 2 Chr 26.4.

[12] Cf Matt 6.2,16,5. Chrysostom is surely being somewhat perverse in thinking only of Jews as being ostentatious in piety and good works.

[13] Chrysostom fails to take psalm titles as (musical) directions to liturgical leaders, as the phrase εἰς τὸ τέλος would suggest (see my introduction to his Commentary on the Psalms, which does not include this psalm). In this case of the title to Ps 57 there is the added obscurity of the phrase μὴ διαφθείρῃς, which a modern commentator like Mitchell Dahood would see as "probably the opening words of a song to whose music the present lament was to be set," coming from Moses' prayer in Deut 9.26 asking God to spare the people. Chrysostom typically takes the flaw inviting final calamity to be sloth, negligence, indifference, ῥᾳθυμία, for which the remedy is προθυμία, enthusiasm: both flaw and remedy lie with us.

[14] Prov 18.3.

[15] Ezek 3.20.

[16] A paraphrase of Ezek 18.21.

[17] 1 Cor 11.17.

[18] 1 Cor 3.17.

[19] Prov 6.30.32 LXX.

[20] With the homily leaving Uzziah at some distance, Chrysostom engages in a digression about the purpose of marriage and, below, a comparison between marriage and virginity – a topic he presented more deliberately and with greater balance in homilies on marriage and (with less balance) in his treatise on virginity.

[21] Chrysostom could expect a well-informed Antiochene listener to this text of Isa 14.14 to claim it is being adduced to imply something other than the author intended (the literal sense of ἀλληγορία), addressed as it is in context not to the devil but to the king of Babylon. It is not a practice Antioch encouraged.

[22] 1 Tim 3.6 in a reading found rarely elsewhere.

[23] Cf Gen 3.5.

[24] Prov 3.34 LXX; cf Jas 4.6; 1 Pet 5.5.

[25] Cf Sir 10.12.

[26] Gen 6.2. Again Uzziah is left behind, as though the preacher is reluctant to stay with his text (he is aware the bishop is to follow). Is there more mileage in sexual morality than in a treatment of pride? Cf note 20 above.

[27] Sir 9.8.

[28] Cf Ps 119.71. Typically, Chrysostom does not spend much time examining the historical context in which Uzziah's arrogance developed, preferring to stress the moral relevance for his listeners, with the aid of other scriptural loci, rooting the vice back – also characteristically – to ῥᾳθυμία.

[29] Ps 131.1.

[30] Giving a brief overview of content is a practice found more frequently in a desk commentator like Theodoret than in the preacher Chrysostom; perhaps on this occasion (apart from the influence of the bishop's presence) he had reason to suspect his congregation might wonder what the homily was really about.

[31] John 4.14.

Homily Four

[1] Questions about the authenticity of this homily are discussed in the introduction. Disorderly behavior by members of the congregation was an issue in Homily One as well. What Chrysostom looks for in his listeners is primarily ὑπακοή – responsiveness, not "docilité" (Dumortier) or *obsequium* (Erasmus).

[2] The agricultural imagery is conventional, of course, typical of Chrysostom but not original, owing something to the evangelical parable (cf Matt 13, e.g.) *inter alia*.

[3] Revelant to the question of authenticity and/or dating of this homily is the appropriateness of this reference to the city's claim to a σύγκλητος – Antioch's or Constantinople's – rivaling Rome's senate.

[4] Cf Gen 18.2.

[5] Cf Matt 3.1.

[6] Sir 25.9.

[7] Matt 5.6.

[8] Chrysostom is flattering his congregation principally for their attentiveness to his homilies; so he proceeds to engage in some word play on the Stoic expression of the human being as a λογικός animal, where λόγος and ἀλογία can mean speech and silence as well as reason and irrationality.

[9] The comparison, extended to Homeric lengths, bears on the preacher's

theme of the importance of homilies, and also highlights the role of the Spirit and Christ as well as the contribution of the homilist, whose tongue is put at their disposition. But at once the homily takes a different turn, sounding the praises of the Church – not a theme generally developed in Chrysostom's OT homilies (in the experience of this translator).

[10] Though some mss omit the catalogue of persecutors, Dumortier is inclined to accept it while seeing the hand of some later author less cultured than Chrysostom in inaccurate description of emperors prior to Nero as persecutors. Augustin, on the other hand, would discount this, seeing the appropriateness of the inclusion of earlier emperors as objects of emperor worship, "people lauded to the skies."

[11] Matt 24.35.

[12] True enough, Homily Three did begin with a promise to discharge a debt, or lay a table, by getting into the story of Uzziah. And though we noted little inroads were made into the story, there was no mention of absentees being the reason. In this fourth homily, however, there is still no anxiety to take up the Uzziah narrative, and as in the third a digression into marriage develops.

[13] Isa 7.3.

[14] One feels that the thesis having been established (not to mention the Uzziah story having been relegated), rhetoric for its own sake has taken over.

[15] 2 Cor 4.18.

[16] Cf Matt 8.16.

[17] Acts 21.9.

[18] John 2.3.

[19] The thesis, that wives who are a liability may prove an asset, is of course even further from the nominal topic for the homily. If it is in fact a homily, women are hardly present to hear this lopsided presentation of wives' (virtues and) vices, followed by the brief acknowledgement of men's similar profile. The moral analysis, however – that not nature but free will is to blame – is thoroughly Antiochene.

[20] This, in fact, was not an issue raised in Homily Three. Cf notes 39 & 40 below.

[21] Chrysostom (and other Antiochenes, like Theodoret) is accustomed to cite the case of these young men as innocent sufferers; but when he mentions the dew that came upon the furnace in Dan 3.49-50, he tends to quote it as a "whistling (διασυρίζον) draft of dew" in the phrasing of the versions in LXX and Theodotion, as in commentary on Pss 111; 139.

[22] Presumably summer heat is proving a problem for the listeners. Chrysostom's biographer, Dom Baur, would see such a reference to conditions in the church as giving "an appearance of actuality" to the text and confirming actual delivery. But from classical times composers have not been above editing a text to convey a sense of spontaneity; see my "Chrysostom's *Commentary on the Psalms*: homilies or tracts?"

[23] Not really the subject of Homily Three, we noted there, despite its title, whereas humility is about to receive belated attention here. For its part, the

title to Homily Four does not adequately describe the contents, either.

[24] Cf Luke 18.11-13.

[25] The point was made in Homily Three, and illustrated there with the analogy of the pirates. The recurrence of this analogy serves Dumortier as one piece of evidence that Homily Four is a pastiche of the other homilies.

[26] Luke 17.10, also quoted in the context of the treatment of arrogance in Homily Three.

[27] Cf Ps 144.4 LXX; 103.15; Isa 40.8.

[28] Matt 16.19.

[29] 2 Chr 26.18.

[30] Num 16.

[31] Cf Num 16.40.

[32] 2 Chr 26.19. In hindsight we read with added pathos this picture of priest obligated to reprove but powerless to secure compliance from ruler armed with military might. Chrysostom was doubtless aware of such situations in living memory, and during his ministry in Constantinople would experience it personally.

[33] Gen 4.12 LXX. Chrysostom elaborates on the text in dramatic fashion, choosing not to mention its reference to the mark on Cain as a preservative, not a punitive, measure.

[34] Cf Exod 20.13.

[35] A cryptic phrase, where Dumortier supplements the text to achieve a meaning, "punishment being the ruin of a good reputation."

[36] Luke 1.20.

[37] Lev 13.46.

[38] In fact, the Isaian verse has received no attention in this homily; it is The Chronicler's story of Uzziah's arrogance that has been to the fore, as also in Homily Three.

[39] 1 Sam 3.1 (not quite the Hebrew or LXX form of the verse), a reference (not, of course to Uzziah's monarchy but) to conditions under the tarnished priesthood of Eli and his rascally sons in the days of the Judges. Unlike its occurrence in Homily Five, Chrysostom transfers the reference of the verse to Uzziah's behavior and its consequence, in the process developing (as a sideline to his basically moral approach to the incident) a further beautiful theology of biblical inspiration as divine communication (ὁμιλία) with human beings. See my "St. John Chrysostom's teaching on inspiration in 'Six homilies on Isaiah'."

[40] Isaiah himself has given Chrysostom no encouragement to draw this inference, nor has The Chronicler; but they are not in a pulpit with a moral agenda.

[41] If the closing doxology takes a somewhat different form, this is hardly unparalleled, nor surprising in view of stenographers' practice, ancient and modern.

Homily Five
[1] The title occurs in various forms in the mss; Dumortier prefers the briefer reading, "On the rest of the Uzziah story."

[2] Luke 14.30.

[3] As we observed in note 38 on Homily Four, Chrysostom did depart from the text of Isaiah to trace Uzziah's story from The Chronicler, as he now admits. It was only in Homily Four, in fact, that he had made the point about Isaiah's ignoring the king's life to focus on his death, something he raises again in this homily.

[4] Dumortier notes that in improving on the scriptural text, Chrysostom has wrongly placed the altar of incense in the Holy of Holies.

[5] Isa 40.6 LXX.

[6] Matt 16.19, a dominical saying not quite bearing on Chrysostom's comparison.

[7] Chrysostom's celebrated treatise on the priesthood was read by Jerome in 392, having been composed (historian Socrates tells us) while he was a deacon, i.e., by 386.

[8] Cf Prov 19.12 LXX.

[9] John 8.34.

[10] 2 Chr 26.18. Chrysostom is no doubt enjoying this prospect of royalty reproved by priesthood.

[11] Wis 2.15: does Chrysostom intend to present the gentle mentor as a "burden" or is he referring here to the abrasive critic? While himself a great admirer of this virtue of πραότης in biblical characters like David and Moses, he did not always excel in its practice in his own ministry, it seems; the correlative, forthrightness, παρρησία, was rather his forte.

[12] Num 16, a text that may not have been on The Chronicler's (or Azariah's) mind; but ἀκρίβεια does not allow the detail to pass unnoticed, and has its own rewards for an Antiochene moralist. Dumortier notes that two separate rebellions – by Dathan and Abiram, and by Korah – have here been combined, the mss and Armenian version opting for one biblical account or other. He might have adverted also to the same combination occurring in Homily Four. For all his ἀκρίβεια, Chrysostom is not one to worry about such niceties; in his Commentary on the Psalms, where Num 16 is cited five times, he can combine the incidents, though also and more frequently citing them separately.

[13] 2 Sam 12.13.

[14] Matt 17.17.

[15] 2 Chr 26.19.

[16] For Dumortier the occurrence of this example of the condemned man with noose in mouth found also in Homily Four is further evidence of the latter's being a pastiche of elements from other homilies, whereas Augustin would say Chrysostom not infrequently reproduces material delivered previously. To be sure, there is definitely an overlap in this homily if it was in fact Homily Four that was the one delivered "the other day," πρώ ην, as he speaks of the interval above; those present then could think provision on this day for the absentees excessive.

[17] Just a passing shot at those with a tendency to kataphatic theology, transgressing the limits of divine transcendence – a concern expressed in Homily Two.

[18] Rom 11.22.
[19] Matt 18.15-17.
[20] This time (cf note 39 on Homily Four) Chrysostom quotes 1 Sam 3.1 more exactly, and admits the reference is to the time of Eli, though applicable also to Uzziah's situation. Divine inspiration of biblical authors is again a casualty of the people's failure.
[21] This point of God's silence being a consequence of the people's failure to expel the leprous Uzziah, on the analogy of someone disappointed in a friend's behavior, occurs also in Homily Four, where it is elaborated.
[22] Cf Hos 11.9.

Homily Six

[1] A title in this form appears in the Armenian version, most mss applying the homily merely "to the seraphim."
[2] Chrysostom begins the first of his two homilies on the obscurity of the Old Testament by speaking of preparation for the "the ocean of Isaiah:" could those homilies have immediately preceded these?
[3] Cf Gal 4.26. Though the homilies are cited under the rubric of Isa 6 for beginning with quotation of the opening verses of that chapter, to this point they have largely been occupied with a moral account of Uzziah's effrontery and the punishment for it as described in 2 Chr 26. Now the preacher wants to return to the more ethereal atmosphere of the Isaian vision, in a manner similar to the opening of Homily Two.
[4] Cf Matt 22.12. While still engaged in lifting the tone of the discourse, Chrysostom has perhaps also in mind the practical need to involve members of the congregation who may have been absent previously or caught up in the kind of distractions he lamented in Homily One.
[5] Prov 22.28. The Isaian passage, of course, rightly discourages kataphatic peering into the vision that the prophet was granted; and an eastern preacher like Chrysostom has had occasion before in these homilies to resist such an approach. He proceeds to set the limits for a commentator on Scripture in the beautiful image of a garment woven of gold, denying himself or any commentator the right to impair the value of the inspired text with his own limited additions (ἀσθένεια – limitations rather than weakness – a key term in his approach to scriptural συγκατάβασις).
[6] Gen 2.18. There is a further inadequate approach to this text on the part of listeners and commentators to be rebutted, a presumption that a seer could not have been married. The preacher had resisted it already in Homily Four by launching into a defense of marriage (the comparison of marriage with virginity in Homily Three – less positive than here – did not arise in this connection).
[7] Isa 6.2 LXX. Chrysostom implies the day's congregation had been present since the beginning of the series.
[8] Matt 18.10.
[9] Matt 18.20.

[10] Ps 34.19.
[11] Col 3.2.
[12] We observed in note 14 on Homily One that Chrysostom, though unwilling to omit comment on this item, misses the euphemism involved, and gives it a different explanation from this attempt, perhaps because of the particular situation he was dealing with there. He seems slightly ill at ease here as well.
[13] Isa 6.3.
[14] Images of emperor and imperial family such as these were, of course, the object of vandalism in the rioting in Antioch in February 387 that led to Chrysostom's Lenten series that year known as the Homilies on the Statues. Does his failure here to advert to that dire event suggest it has not yet occurred? Dumortier would see the series concluded by early 387, Tillemont would postpone Homily Six till after Lent 387, Montfaucon dating Homily Six to a few days before Lent, possibly 388 (mention of the approach of Lent occurring in the text below; see note 18).
[15] Chrysostom expects his congregation to recognize this refrain (the Sanctus in the Latin liturgy) from the eucharistic ritual, and he proceeds to give the passage a eucharistic interpretation, so that it becomes in fact a profound study of this sacrament. In the course of it he mentions Christ's removal of the dividing wall, as does Eph 2.14-15 (though the two groups in that case are Jew and Gentile), and making peace, as do Eph and Col 1.20 (the latter referring to heaven and earth); and he proceeds to refer implicitly to passages about worship from Rom (e.g., 12.1) and Heb. These New Testament echoes encourage him to recognize a typological meaning in the Isaian verses.
[16] Isa 6.6.
[17] The reference here, Dumortier believes, is to reception of the eucharistic species in the hand of the communicant (is Chrysostom referring to the eucharistic species as "this spiritual fire"?). The following sentence, for which Dumortier accepts the distinctive reading of the Armenian, basically involves a contrast between the dignity of the offering and the συγκατάβασις of the offerer.
[18] Lent, a period extended to eight weeks in the eastern church at that time (Saturday and Sunday being exempt), began on March 1 in 387 (the imperial portraits were vandalised on February 27; see note 14 and the introduction to the Homilies on Hannah).
[19] Chrysostom's term is κοινωνία, which may be rendered by "sharing, fellowship," and as "communion" suggests directly the eucharistic sacrament (cf 1 Cor 10.16). He has moved on from the seraphim to the Christian eucharist, μυστήρια. He is also employing the terminology of the Games: prizes are won in the (jumping) pits, σκάμμα, and the length of the race track, στάδιον, has been extended (to an eight-week Lent).
[20] Chrysostom may be referring to the Easter vigil, or simply recalling parabolic scenes of banquets and vigils (e.g., Matt 22.2-14; 25.1-13).
[21] Luke 18.13.
[22] Chrysostom (and other Antiochene pastors) can struggle to come up

with a sound balance between the roles of divine grace and human effort in the process of salvation and spiritual development, the latter element often receiving greater emphasis. Here by contrast he goes out of his way to express the priority of the former.

[23] Isa 49.15.

[24] Gen 27.13.

[25] Gal 3.13.

[26] Cf Mark 9.47-48. The preacher, like many another, has strayed from the topic, the seraphim of Isa 6, to the holiness of the eucharist, the need for proper dispositions in its reception, the prior role of God's love, and the inappropriateness of lack of response. It is time to retrace his steps.

[27] Heb 10.31.

[28] Though in fact the term συγκατάβασις, considerateness, did not occur earlier (hence, perhaps, Dumortier's choosing here the reading φιλανθρωπία of the Armenian), we found it in note 17 an adequate term – and typical of Chrysostom – for expressing the divine acceptance of human limitations in Christ's exercise of priesthood dwelt on there.

[29] It is certainly an accurate and comprehensive summary of Homily Six. Does the fact that the preacher makes no attempt to survey and summarize all the homilies confirm the impression of some commentators that this homily was delivered well after the others? But cf note 7.

[30] Can we conclude from this parenetic formula that women, children and servants were not present for this homily (or normally for any others)?

[31] Cf Exod 23.4-5.

[32] Cf 2 Cor 5.10.

General Index

Aaron, 90, 91, 99
Abiram, 90, 99, 101, 131
Abraham, 22, 32, 33, 56, 64, 80, 84, 126
Achan, 57, 58, 124, 125
actuality, 117, 129
ἀκρίβεια, 5, 23, 43, 117, 120, 121, 122, 123, 126, 131
allegory, 44, 128
Allen, P., 116
almsgiving, 121
angel, 106
Anomeans, 42, 125
Antioch, *passim*
anthropomorphism, 23, 120
Arian, 117, 126
arrogance, 6, 75-79, 88, 89, .91, 92, 94, 96, 130
Aubineau, M., 115, 119, 120
Augustin, P., 115, 129, 131
Augustine, 117

ban, 57, 58, 59, 125
baptism, 123
Barthélemy, D., 115
Baur, C., 115, 117, 129
bishop, 20, 21, 23, 41, 45, 117, 126, 127, 128
Bouyer, L., 115
byzantine, 3, 120

catenae, 1
church, 46, 47, 60, 80, 81, 83, 84, 123, 129
Constantinople, 20, 21, 24, 118, 119, 120, 128, 130
context, 10-13
council, 117
creation, 25-29
creed, 1
Cyrus, 24, 122

Dahood, M., 127
Dathan, 90, 91, 99, 101, 131
David, *passim*
deacon, 131
διδασκαλεῖον, 20
Diocletian, 127,
Diodore of Tarsus, 22, 44, 119
Drewery, B., 115
dualism, 119
Dumortier, J., 115, 122, 123, 125, 126, 127, 129, 130, 131, 133, 134

Easter, 132
Eli, 42, 102, 130, 132
emperor, 55, 82, 124, 129, 133
eucharist, 20, 41, 109, 110, 123, 124, 133, 134
exegesis, 3, 42, 118, 120
Eunomian, 126
Eustathius, 3, 7, 117
evil, 121, 122

Fall, 44
fasting, 109-110
Fernández Marcos, N., 115
Flavian, 126, 127
Fronto de Duc, 119

grace, 5, 117, 118, 134

Hebrew, 1, 126, 130
heretic, 21, 25
hermeneutics, 1, 22, 23, 44, 121
Hill, R. C., 15, 116, 117, 122, 123, 129, 130

inspiration, 2, 43, 81, 93-94, 102, 103, 117, 122, 123, 125, 126, 130, 132

Jerome, 117, 131
Jews, 14, 22, 38, 66, 82, 83, 126, 127
Job, 22, 32, 40, 86, 121

kataphatic, 123, 125, 132
Kelly, J. N. D., 116
Korah, 90, 99, 101, 131

Latin, 133
Law, 37
Lazarus, 22, 32, 33
lectionary, 13, 43
Lent, 20, 41, 45, 133
Leroux, J.-M., 116
literalist, 119
liturgy, 1, 5, 20, 21, 23, 41, 43, 117, 119, 120, 123, 127, 133

Maccabees, 84
manichees, 21, 119

manuscript, 119, 125, 129
marriage, 11, 12, 80, 83-86, 105, 127, 129, 132
martyr, 3, 7, 127
Mayer, W., 116
Mountfaucon, B. de, 21, 23, 117, 119, 122, 124, 127, 133
morality, 1, 4, 22, 41, 118, 128, 130, 131, 132
moralizing, 122
Moses, 56, 57, 84, 92, 127, 131
music, 127
mysticism, 44

Nebuchadnezzar, 14
Nicea, 117
norms, 5, 18, 119
Novatian, 123

obscurity, 41, 126, 132
Olympic, 109
Origen, 117

παχύτης, 23, 120, 123
pastoral, 1
Paul, *passim*
pelagian, 11
penitential, 123
Peter, 3, 7, 8, 18, 85, 117
physician, 98, 118
poverty, 31-35, 121
πραότης, 131
prayer, 124
priest, 84, 89-90, 95, 96-97, 99, 100, 130, 131, 134
προθυμία, 117, 127
προφῆται, 1, 126

races, 20, 119

Rad, G. von, 116
ῥᾳθυμία, 5, 8, 44, 104, 117, 118, 121, 127, 128
rationalizing, 23, 124, 117, 121, 122
repentance, 103, 110-112
riches, 31-35
rigorism, 123
Romanus, 3, 7
Rome, 80, 119, 128

sacrament, 112123, 124, 133
Sancta Eirene, 21, 119
Sancta Sophia, 21, 119
Savile, H., 21
Schäublin, C., 116
senate, 80, 128
seraphim, *passim*
Septuagint, 1, 129, 130
Socrates Scholasticus, 131
soteriology, 121
spectacles, 55, 123
spirituality, 1, 117, 125, 134
Statues, 20, 133
stenography, 130
Stoic, 128
συνάξεις, 119, 123, 124
συγκατάβασις, 41, 42, 123, 125, 132, 133, 134

Ternant, P., 116
theatre, 95
Theodore of Mopsuestia, 120
Theodoret of Cyrus, 1, 120, 121, 128, 129
Theodotion, 129
theology, 117, 126
theôria, 44, 124

Tillemont, L., 21, 24, 133
transcendence, 22, 122, 32
trinitarian, 123
typology, 44, 124, 133

ὑπακοή, 21, 119, 123, 128
Uzziah, *passim*

Vaccari, A., 116
virginity, 4, 11, 127, 132
vocation, 2

Wallace-Hadrill, D. S., 116
widowhood, 4, 11, 12
wife, 83-86, 105, 129
women, 4, 134

Young, F. M., 116

Index of Biblical Citations

Old Testament
in gen., 1, 2, 41

Genesis
1.26, 118
2.18, 132
2.20, 126
3.5, 128
4.12, 130
6.2, 128
17.5, 126
18.2, 128
27.13, 134
49.10

Exodus
20.13, 130
23.4-5, 134

Leviticus
13.46, 130

Numbers
16, 130131
16.40, 130

Deuteronomy
7.3-4, 124

Joshua
6.17-18, 124

7.1-5, 124
7.10-12, 124
7.20-21, 124
7.24-25, 124

1 Samuel
3.1, 42, 130, 132

2 Samuel
12.13, 131

1 Kings
17.1, 121

2 Chronicles
26, 41, 45
26.4, 127
26.15-16, 126, 127
26.18, 130
26.19, 127, 130, 131

Psalms
1.21, 121
2.11, 123
4.7, 121
10.11, 2, 118
10.13, 3, 118
12.6, 126
14.1, 3, 118
19, 21
19.1, 120

19.2-3, 120
34.19, 133
34.21, 121
51.17, 124
57, 127
66.1, 124
103.15, 130
104.24, 21, 120
111, 129
116.15, 121
119.71, 128
127.1, 3, 4, 117
131.1, 128
137, 21, 119
137.1-3, 121
139, 129
144.4, 130
148.14, 125

Proverbs
3.34, 128
6.30-32, 127
9.9, 121
18.3, 127
19.12, 131
22.28, 132

Ecclesiastes
3.2, 23, 121
3.4, 23, 121
3.7, 126

Wisdom of Solomon
2.15, 131

Sirach
1.1-2, 119
2.10, 118

7.5, 127
9.8, 128
10.12, 128
23.11, 124
25.9, 128

Isaiah
1.19-20, 119
6, 2, 41-113, 125
6.1, 122, 125
6.2, 132
6.3, 123, 125, 133
6.6, 133
7.3, 129
7.20, 123
14.14, 44, 128
40.6, 131
40.8, 129
43.26, 127
44.24, 24
45.6-7, 1, 20-41, 118, 119, 120
49.15, 134
66.2, 125

Jeremiah
6.14, 122
7.16, 118
10.19-22, 118
10.23, 1, 2-19, 20, 21, 23, 118
10.24, 118

Ezekiel
3.20, 127
18, 124

Daniel
3.49-50, 129
10.8-9

Amos
3.6, 121, 122

Jonah
3.4, 122

Haggai
2.8, 3, 4, 118

Matthew
3.1, 128
5.6, 128
5.16, 120
6.2, 127
6.5, 127
6.34, 122
8.16, 129
9.20-22, 21, 120
11.28, 123
13, 128
16.19, 130, 131
17.17, 131
18.10, 133
18.15-17, 132
18.20, 133
20.6-7, 118
22.2-14, 132, 133
23.3-7, 118
24.35, 129
25.1-13, 133
25.14-36, 45, 124, 125

Mark
9.47-48, 124

Luke
1.20, 130
14.30, 131
17.10, 127, 130

18.10-14, 118, 130, 134
22.31-32, 119

John
2.3, 129
2.10, 126
4.14, 128
5.43, 126
6.66, 119
8.21, 124
8.34, 131

Acts
10.34-35, 119
11.19-26, 117
21.9, 129

Romans
5.5, 119
9.16, 3, 4, 117
11.22, 132
12.1, 133

1 Corinthians
3.17, 127
10.13, 119
10.16, 133
11.17, 127
14, 123

2 Corinthians
4.18, 129
5.10, 134
6, 21, 120
6.4-5, 120
7.10, 121
11, 21, 120
11.23-27, 120

Galatians
2.11, 17
3.13, 134
4.19, 125
4.26, 132
5.22, 117

Ephesians
2.14-15, 133

Philippians
1.22-24, 121
4.4, 121

Colossians
1.20, 133
3.2, 133

1 Thessalonians
2.7, 125

2 Thessalonians
3.10, 121

1 Timothy
3.6, 44, 128
5.11-12, 118
5.23, 121

Hebrews
10.31, 134

James
4.6, 128
5.16, 124

1 Peter
5.5, 128